Essay on time

*A brief study of the representation of time
in religion and magic*

DURKHEIM PRESS

editors W. S. F. Pickering and W. Watts Miller

TITLES

Emile Durkheim, *Montesquieu / Quid Secundatus Politicae Scientiae Instituendae Contulerit*

Henri Hubert, *Essay on Time*

Mark Cladis, ed., *Durkheim and Foucault: perspectives on education and punishment*

Marcel Mauss, *Prayer* (forthcoming)

Essay on time

A brief study of the representation of time in religion and magic

Henri Hubert

edited by Robert Parkin
translated by Robert Parkin and Jacqueline Redding

DURKHEIM PRESS

OXFORD

© **Durkheim Press Ltd 1999**

First published in 1999 by Durkheim Press Ltd
PO Box 889, Oxford OX2 6GP

Printed and bound by Antony Rowe Ltd
Chippenham, Wiltshire SN14 6LH

A CIP record for this book is available from
the British Library

ISBN: 978-0-95299-361-2

CONTENTS

The initiative for this publication comes from our colleague, Robert Parkin, who, several years ago, began to translate Hubert's essay on time. He realised, as we all do, that in many ways the essay was unique and was on a subject that over the years has been forgotten until recently — time considered anthropologically.

Presenting this essay, now translated for the first time into English, raises at least two problems by way of introduction. The first is to offer some commentary on the essay itself in pointing to its salient features. The second is to introduce to English-speaking readers something of the life and work of Henri Hubert, who was a member of the Année Sociologique group. We found both these requirements were to be had in an article by the French sociologist and specialist in religion, F.-A. Isambert. We are grateful to him for his permission to translate the article, which has been slightly edited, to serve as a direct introduction to Hubert's essay.

The production of what is here the second book to be published by the Durkheim Press has been achieved through the assistance of several people. In the first instance thanks are due to the pioneer of the book, Bob Parkin. The services of Jacqueline Redding, in carrying out a great deal of the translation, have been invaluable. Her husband, Ian Redding, is also thanked for his advice in coping with scientific terms. Further assistance has come from Carol Pickering who undertook the typing of much of the manuscript and of sub-editing it.

W.S.F. Pickering
W. Watts Miller

1

Henri Hubert (1872-1927) vers 1910.

INTRODUCTION*

François-André Isambert

1 Life and Work of Henri Hubert (1872-1927)

At the point where the sociology of religion and the sociology of knowledge meet, Henri Hubert's "Etude sommaire de la représentation du temps dans la religion et la magie" impressed me long ago as a penetrating work. Given the opportunity to look more closely at the genesis of the fundamental ideas of the Durkheimian school,[1] I realised that the study occupied a strategic position in this development, also that Henri Hubert's rôle had undoubtedly played an essential part in the refining of ideas which Durkheim was to systematise in *The Elementary Forms of Religious Life*.

Paradoxically, it would seem that Hubert's reputation has suffered from his collaboration, if not his friendship with Marcel Mauss.[2] The tendency has been to give most credit to the latter for their joint "Essai sur la nature et la fonction du sacrifice" and their "Esquisse d'une théorie générale de la magie". As for his "Etude sommaire de la représentation du temps dans la religion et la magie", who thinks of attributing it to him since it was republished in the *Mélanges d'histoire des religions* under the names of Hubert and Mauss?[3] Yet, if we include his many articles,

* Translated Jacqueline Redding from F-A. Isambert, "Henri Hubert et la sociologie du temps", *Revue française de sociologie*, XX, 1, 1979: 182-204.

notes and reviews, Henri Hubert's work is at least as voluminous as that of Mauss.[4] Hubert's share of the essays written jointly with Mauss, his introduction to Chantepie de la Saussaye's *Manuel d'histoire des religions*, his "Etude sommaire sur la représentation du temps" and his "Culte des héros et ses conditions sociales", to mention only the chief ones, are far from being minor contributions to French sociology. We must also count the sociological inspiration which informed his work as a prehistorian and historian of the religions of pre-Christian Europe.

It is important then, at a time when we are becoming aware of the richness of the sociological work of the Durkheimians other than Durkheim himself and Mauss, and of the impact they had on Durkheim's thought, to publicise the work of Henri Hubert. Rather than a simple biographical article, we need a comprehensive study of his entire work and I would welcome a thesis which applied itself to this task. It is time that the projected edition of Hubert's works — his sociological works at least — should see the light of day.[5] My contribution to these anticipated projects will be twofold. To begin with, I shall prepare the ground for an intellectual biography of Hubert. Later on, I shall analyse what it was that demonstrated to me the merit of Hubert's thought, namely, his study of time.

2 Sociologist, historian, archaeologist

Born into a family of the Parisian bourgeoisie[6] and to a father who had retired from business early, Henri Hubert gravitated towards history at the time of his studies at the Lycée Louis-le-Grand, where the school chaplain, Abbé

Quentin, helped to awaken in him a taste for the history of religions. As a student at the Ecole Normale Supérieure, *agrégé* in history, Hubert's university life took the accepted path. He turned towards research, however, rather than towards a career in teaching. In 1895 he specialised in the history of religions and philosophy. He attended courses at the Ecole Pratique des Hautes Etudes and in the fourth and then in the fifth section followed the courses of A. Carrière, V. Scheil, J. Halévy, V. Bérard, S. Lévi and I. Levi, and V. Derenbourg. In those days Celtic history and oriental languages seemed to interest him in equal measure. It was at that time that he became friends with Marcel Mauss and they both collaborated on the first issue of *L'Année sociologique*, published in 1898. In this first issue he was only responsible, along with Mauss, for the section under the heading of *Mythes* and the only review signed by him was also signed by Mauss. But in the second issue, he became jointly responsible for almost all the headings in the section *Sociologie religieuse* and put his name to about twenty reviews. Even more importantly he published with Mauss the famous "Essai sur la nature et la fonction du sacrifice" (1899). His contributions permeated the first and second series of *L'Année sociologique*.[7]

Meanwhile, since 1898, he had been working as a general assistant at the Musée des Antiquités Nationales at Saint-Germain-en-Laye, where he became assistant curator in 1910. In 1901, he had gone to the Ecole des Hautes Etudes as a lecturer in the department of religious sciences, specializing in the primitive religions of Europe. He was to retain this post until his death,[8] apart from a break from 1914 to 1919 on account of the war. Finally, from 1906 onwards, he taught national archaeology at the Ecole du Louvre, which he also continued to do until the end of his life. Both at Saint-Germain and at the Ecole du Louvre, his duties brought him into close contact with Salomon Reinach, whose erudition he valued but whose sectarianism he criticised.[9] Whilst the majority of his archaeological writings appear to be linked to his duties at the museum at Saint-Germain, his specifically historical and sociological work bears the marks of his teaching.

His first important publication[10] was of a historical nature. Using the *Liber Pontificalis* which had been analyzed by Abbé Louis Duchesne (the future Monseigneur Duchesne who would be accused of modernism), he sought to assess the rôle of politics and religion in the Iconoclastic Controversy which resulted in the formation of the States of the Church in the eighth century.

The best known part of Hubert's whole work is what he wrote with Mauss, namely, the "Essai sur la nature et la fonction du sacrifice" and the "Esquisse d'une théorie générale de la magie". It would no doubt be pointless to speak of the individual contribution of each of the two collaborators and contrary to the very spirit of their collaboration. As far as the "Essai sur la nature et la fonction du sacrifice" is concerned, an autobiographical note left by Hubert at the time of the First World War[11] makes one aspect of his contribution clear. His thesis on the Syrian goddess[12] had led him to a particular consideration of the sacrifice of the god, and the articulation typical of the rite and the myth which it represents. It constituted a theme which, as is well known, took up the whole of the last part of the essay. More significantly, Hubert's dual competence in Greek and Roman history and in Semitic studies (Judaic, Assyro–Babylonian), useful for clarifying bibliographical facts, is well attested by the many reviews in these fields he wrote for *L'Année sociologique*. Mauss, who was far from being ignorant in this area, was none the less more inclined towards India, and also towards so-called "primitive" peoples (especially those of Australia). In this way, we can up to a certain point, discriminate between their respective areas of competence.

But at most, this only allows us to divide up the bibliographical references. In so far as the actual development is concerned, nothing entitles us to think that Hubert's rôle was a subordinate one. In the note already referred to, Hubert himself speaks of their shared thought:

> The problems which confronted us are as follows: the nature of religious phenomena, the conditions of the religious phenomenon, the nature and conditions of the myth. They did not present themselves in the abstract: their particular position gave rise to our work on myth and on magic.... In the analysis of religious facts, the examination of the representations which preside over their development and determine their logic seemed to be the first priority. We singled out the idea of the sacred: we saw it as a category of the mental operations implied by religious facts.[13]

If proof were needed of the active participation of Hubert in their joint thought, it would be sufficient to look at the intellectual vigour displayed in his own individual publications, whether it be in *L'Année sociologique*, in the introduction to Chantepie de La Saussaye, or in the "Etude sommaire de la représentation du temps". Through these various works, we see him systematically pursuing the question of the origin and social variations of "mental categories", a question we shall have to return to. But we must not overstate our case. Whilst the idea, a debatable one in any case, of the sacred as category is notably developed by Hubert in the introduction to Chantepie, the problem of the social character of categories is also raised by Durkheim and Mauss in "De quelques Formes primitives de classification".[14] In fact, it would seem that what we have here, is evidence of a collective discussion in which Hubert plays his part along with the others, whether the score requires him to play a duet or a solo.

It is in the same spirit that we must interpret the degree of his involvement in "Esquisse d'une théorie générale de la magie". The abundance of facts relating to archaic cultures would indicate the predominance of Mauss, but at that very time Hubert was publishing a long article, "Magia", in the *Dictionnaire des antiquités grecques et romaines*. Anybody can see at this juncture that the article is entirely documentary and barely systematic, that the sociological theory of magic is hardly discernible, and that Hubert's contribution to the common effort on magic risks being of the same kind. Bearing in mind what has just been said, there is, on the contrary, every reason to believe that in some sense, Hubert put into this article the excess of documentation he was unable to include in the "Esquisse d'une théorie générale de la magie". Besides, it shows a characteristic of Hubert's work taken as a whole: the alternation between theoretical works and others where theory scarcely obtrudes and takes second place to erudition.

On this subject of collaboration, it must not be forgotten that when Hubert and Mauss published the *Mélanges d'histoire des religions* under their joint names, the "Etude sommaire de la représentation du temps" was presented as work in common which fortuitous circumstances alone had necessitated publication under the name of Hubert.[15] In similar fashion, "L'Origine des pouvoirs magiques dans les sociétés australiennes" was published under the name of Mauss for the same reasons.[16] It is certain that these two works were published at the time of the greatest collaboration between the two men. Each must therefore bear the traces — more even — of the thought of both authors. Each none the less, was published as being the responsibility of the named writer. Whereas in 1906 their friendship led them to present these as communal works, some years previously Mauss had reviewed the work of his friend in *L'Année sociologique* as being his own individual work, and had not hesitated to criticise it.[17] Even more conclusive is the fact that the "Etude sommaire de la représentation du temps" reworks a course of lectures given by Hubert at the Ecole des Hautes Etudes, serving as an introduction to his seminar on the calendar and the festivals of the Germans. It is, therefore, justifiable to believe it to be Hubert's own work, without denying Mauss's share in the thought which inspired it. This work is indeed a seminal text in French sociology.

On the other hand, nobody contests Hubert's authorship of the introduction to the French translation of Chantepie de la Saussaye's *Manuel d'histoire des religions*.[18] Of course, he did not imagine that he was writing an original work, but attempting a synthesis of the contributions made by what he termed "the French school" of sociology, to religious subjects. Now, it so happens that no one seems to have noticed that, after Durkheim's article in *L'Année sociologique*, "De la Définition des phénomènes religieux",[19] the "Essai sur la nature et la fonction du sacrifice" and the "Esquisse d'une théorie générale de la magie", this introduction was the first Durkheimian synthesis of a sociology of religion. In it is to be found Durkheim's criticism of Max Müller and Réville, but on the other hand it also includes an expression of gratitude to the English school of anthropology, described as "the penultimate school of the science of religions".[20] What is more significant, and very characteristic of Hubert as we shall see, is his claim of a continuity between the notion of the *collective*, a key word of the new school and the notion of the *popular*, a vague, ill-defined but very fruitful idea. At one and the same time it pointed the way to the study of popular religion which Hubert undertook along with Hertz and Czarnowski, and acknowledged the Germanic contributions of the *Völkerpsychologie* and the *Volkskunde*.[21]

There are many things in this work which may appear banal and yet it marked a decisive stage for the Durkheimian school. It is in the precise points which follow that Hubert displayed his originality.[22] First is the subtle analysis of the modalities of religion in all their diversity, as opposed to the often oversimplifying schematisation of Durkheim. When we speak of the Roman, Greek or Assyrian religion, the word does not have the same meaning as in speaking of Buddhism, Islam or Christianity. The latter are "systems of institutions, acts and thoughts which appear to be more or less defined and consciously ordered": they are what are called "churches". The others are "very loose, very vague systems, whose unity, albeit real, remains altogether theoretical": they are what the author calls a "religion of peoples".[23] Merging can occur between the realities of the two orders, such that whereas in Judaism, the church and the people coincide, in the Far East the case is quite different. Here, elements of religious systems and even churches interpenetrate to the extent of co-existing, not only in the same peoples, but even in the same individuals. To these two relatively systematized orders, we must add those "myths and diverse beliefs which do not seem to belong to any system", which are studied in folklore and to which Hubert attaches special importance.

It should be noted that to the first, essentially coercive conception of religion in Durkheim, Hubert adds an affective conception — in the same sense as in the "Esquisse d'une théorie générale de la magie" — thereby putting in place the collective affectivity which for Durkheim will be — in *The Elementary Forms of Religious Life* — at the heart of religion. It is in this direction that we find the theory of the soul as individual mana, condensed from the collective mana, or according to Hubert, where several collective mana meet. This will be taken up later by Durkheim more or less as he found it.

Still, there is no need to stress once more the fact that it was with Hubert's introduction to Chantepie de la Saussaye that the Durkheimian school marked the watershed in its sociology of religion and progressed towards a definition based on the sacred.[24] The notion of the sacred itself however, is no longer only that of the interdict, or of the property which entails that interdict. It is something much more encompassing and by virtue of that, determining. From the point of view of the object, it is an "environment" of which the "Essai sur la nature et la fonction du sacrifice" has given some idea. It is an environment "which one enters into and emerges from" and whose nature regulates the operations taking place within it. From the point of view of the intellect, it is a sort of "category". This notion of category in relation to sacred time will be considered later on. Suffice it to say for the moment that Hubert's aim is to make us understand that the sacred acts "by imposing conditions on experience and on reasoning".[25] In other words, the sacred which in practice presents itself as the general form of constraints operating on ritual behaviour, appears in the consciousness as the general form of constraints operating on religious thought.

But, just as Hubert had been aware of the multiplicity of the forms of religion, so too, for him the sacred was not monolithic. He would demonstrate this several years later along with Czarnowski, in thinking about the hero. Stefan Czarnowski, who was a Polish pupil of Hubert, had in fact written a study of *Saint Patrick, héros nationale de l'Irlande*.[26] The text was ready in 1913. Hubert went over it carefully and wrote a long preface, virtually a book in itself. In 1914-1915, he submitted lengthy extracts to the *Revue historique*. The war delayed publication of the work which had to wait until 1919.

To begin with, Hubert questioned in detail the alleged value of Czarnowski's work which, he considered, offered the double paradox for a Durkheimian of not utilising the comparative method, but rather of producing an extended monograph, and yet attempting to proceed from that to a theory of the hero. The difficulty is compounded by the fact that Saint Patrick is not a "pure" hero but a saint functioning as a hero, thereby posing a formidable typological problem. Now, it is obvious that basically Hubert has a preference for Czarnowski's methodological heterodoxy. When contrasting the works which begin with theories as their starting–point and those which start from odd facts that are read as theoretical questions, we can see that he prefers the latter. This contrast is not unrelated to the distinction he makes between sociologist–philosophers and sociologist–historians.[27] Be that as it may, two problems pose themselves: to what social type does the hero correspond? How can we delineate the process of heroisation?

Regarding the first point, Hubert meticulously examines Czarnowski's attempt to define the hero and like him demonstrates all the ambiguity which normally surrounds the term. In particular, the semi-divine character usually ascribed to the hero clouds the issue, and the combination of hero and saint has the same effect. There is no doubt that as an intermediary personage, and participating in the sacred, the hero must be firmly placed on the side of men. Unlike kings who easily become gods to the extent that they have divine right, heroes have "human right". In the rôle of figurehead, they embody the community itself and not some power which could be favourable or inimical to it. This removes a Durkheimian ambiguity which, taking the totem as a prototype for the divinity, leads us to believe — without actually saying so — that every god is some sort of evolved totem. Moreover, Hubert notes very explicitly the functional relationship of the totem and the hero, whilst leaving open the question of the actual connection between the one and the other. In the case of Ireland, a country of clans, the totemic function of the hero is especially evident. The hero is the real or mythical ancestor of the clan. When specifically religious groups set themselves up in a comparable structure (dioceses, monasteries), saints play the part of religious heroes, not because they are saints but because they are founders. When the clans and the religious groups converge together in a church which at the same time links the clans at a national level, we have Saint Patrick, a national saint and hero.

This brilliant demonstration nevertheless leaves Hubert dissatisfied because what seems to him to be the most interesting thing in Czarnowski, is the beginning of an analysis of the process of heroisation. But as this is barely outlined, Hubert feels compelled to take it further. How does one become a hero? This question is transformed by contact with the problem of the relationship between the rite and the myth. The problem posed is to know at the heart of which ritual practice the figure of the hero develops — not that Hubert argues for a systematic pre-existence of rite over myth. But he posits "the intertwining of rites and myths, their reciprocal influences, their reaction to each other".[28] Some have seen in the sacrifice of the hero and his commemoration the cultic foundation of the heroic legend. Here, Hubert distinguishes clearly between the sacrifice of the god which recurs, and the death of the hero which is commemorated. Hybrid or doubtful examples are always of course, possibilities.[29] In similar fashion he separates mimetic rites and sacred dramas. Finally, it is the festival itself which supports the heroisation, at least the festival as analysed by Durkheim in *The Elementary Forms of Religious Life*, combining a religious ceremony with entertainment. This mixed character corresponds directly with the intermediate character of the hero. Hubert goes on to emphasize the familiar, sometimes comic, traits of the hero, contrasting him or her with the saint.

It is difficult in a few lines to convey the impression of fidelity to the facts in all their complexity given by Hubert's analysis of the information at his disposal. It is equally difficult to convey his instinct for the changes, intermediate states, and combinations which provided him with the only means of simultaneously being faithful to the extraordinary breadth of his erudition and his desire to theorise. Perhaps we should regret the occasional tendency towards essentialism which he shared with his Durkheimian companions. There is absolutely no doubt in Hubert's mind that the hero exists as a social type along with the festival whose function is commemorative. Unconsciously, this may well be after all a fertile concession on the part of the sociologist–historian to the sociologist–philosophers.

It would misrepresent Hubert's intellectual personality if we were to detach his work as a historian–archaeologist from his sociological work. As a historian of religions he was fed by archaeology as well as by the study of texts. This is shown in his long articles on "Kyrèné"(1900) and on "Nantosuelta, déesse de la ruche" (1912a), or again his analysis "Une nouvelle Figure du dieu au maillet"(1915), or his last article, "De quelques Objets de bronze trouvés à Byblos" (1925). These studies alternate between those on the ancient Near East and those dealing with Celtic material. In its turn, the history of religions nourished his sociology, as witnessed by Mauss who saw in him one of the only two mythologists that sociology could command.[30] The unity of his thought was given concrete expression in a few major syntheses which emerged from the multitude of meticulously detailed works. At the time of his death, he was preparing an *Ethnographie préhistorique de l'Europe*.[31] It would seem that he left behind him at Saint-Germain a quite outstanding body of material tracing the technological history of humanity.[32]

In all probability his death was hastened by sorrow. In 1910 he had married a woman of German nationality by whom he had a son in 1913. The war came along and he was called up. He was recalled from the front in 1915 and posted to the Ministry of Armaments to work with Albert Thomas. Durkheim's death affected him greatly. But worse, in 1924 he lost his wife as she gave birth to a second son. What was the exact cause of his death? All we know is that for several years he struggled on in the attempt to complete the work he had undertaken.[33]

Hubert left several unfinished works: the thesis on the Syrian goddess which was referred to in his intellectual testament of 1915, but which has now disappeared without trace, a half–finished work on the Celts, based on his course on Celtic archaeology at the Ecole du Louvre and another on the Germans, the subject of his course at the Ecole des Hautes Etudes. Each of these two works had been promised to Henri Berr for inclusion in his collection "L'Evolution de l'humanité", but their subsequent history turned out to be very different.

The text of *Les Celtes* had been prepared long before: the main part of the work, according to Hubert's own admission, had been completed in 1914 (letter of 15 June 1919).[34] He had taken it up again on returning from the war and had finished a first version in January 1923. Hubert's conscientious temperament however led him to "revise the whole, to cut, to join up again and to verify".[35] Battling against illness in the two last years, he constantly believed that he was nearing the end of his exertions. On Thursday, 26 May 1927, a note from Marcel Mauss informed Henri Berr of the death of their friend. "The manuscript of *Les Celtes* was on his table: he was working on it on Tuesday."[36] Marcel Mauss, Raymond Lantier and Jean Marx took charge of the text. Joseph Vendryès re-read the chapters on linguistics. The material for a first volume was more or less ready. It remained to check the quotations, to bring the references up to date, and *Les Celtes et l'expansion celtique jusqu'à l'époque de la Tène* appeared in February 1932. A year later, *Les Celtes depuis l'époque de la Tène et la civilisation celtique* came out.[37] Each of the two volumes included a preface by H. Berr which was omitted in the 1974 edition. The first volume (1932a) contained a foreword by Marcel Mauss. We are told that the second part of the book had not been drafted, but that a thoroughly comprehensive lecture course enabled Lantier and Mauss to write up what was missing.

As far as the third part is concerned, things were different. "It had comprised", wrote Mauss, "the subject–matter of a lengthy course lasting a year. The present work however, even when published in two volumes, would have been too long for inclusion in the collection 'L'Evolution de l'humanité' — certainly if the admirable lectures prepared by Hubert for the purpose had been published as they stood".[38]

Hubert's friends decided on the "horrendous task" of "summarising in two chapters" this year–long course, thereby keeping the promise Hubert had made to Henri Berr. Jean Marx and Raymond Lantier carried out the work expecting the course would be published *in extenso* — something which never happened.[39] The "horrendous task" in fact produced five chapters which would repay prolonged study. Suffice it to say that they constitute the prototype for what one might call "archaeo–sociology" with a chapter on "Objet et méthode d'une étude sociologique des Celtes", two more on "La Structure de la société celtique", one on space and time, and finally "Activités sociales": economics and technology, art and literature. It will be noted that here religion is not taken as being a particular "activité", but is studied in relation to the structure as a whole.

The text of *Les Germains* was apparently nearer its final state. At least, Paul Chalus was able to publish a faithful version of the content, lecture by lecture, of a course left by Hubert, by working from an almost complete text and bridging the gaps with the help of course notes.[40] Publication however, did not take place until 1952! In *Les Celtes* Mauss had already heralded the publication of *Les Germains*. But one of Hubert's pupils was put in charge of editing the text and nothing more was heard of it until 1950, when it re-surfaced because of two unexpected discoveries.

A manuscript version was found among Mauss's papers at his death, and a typewritten text appeared in a cupboard which had belonged to Hubert's former pupil.[41] It seems that Mauss had intended to add to *Les Germains*. Indeed, while Hubert had for many years devoted courses to the *Les Germains* at the Ecole des Hautes Etudes, the book in question is essentially tied to the problem of origins. That is to say that there is relatively little here on civilization and society. In the course which had preceded the publication of the "Etude sommaire de la représentation du temps", we know that Hubert had studied the Germanic calendar and, in a wider sense, time among the Germans. Turning now to the essay on time does not mean losing sight of the Germans.

3 Social Time

The "Etude sommaire de la représentation du temps" appears in the first instance to be the response to a relatively limited problem, albeit one which is central to the sociology of religion. The difficulty was expressed succinctly in *L'Année sociologique*: "Given that in fact religious acts take place in space and time, one of the enigmas of ritual is the reconciliation of these inescapable conditions with the infinite extent and the theoretical immutability of the sacred. Ritual must consequently bring into play representations and figurations of space and time necessary to resolve this antinomy".[42]

So expressed, the problem seems to refer to one of those tricks which rites are full of and whose aim is to reconcile the irreconcilable: the high and the low, hot and cold, life and death. On closer inspection, however, the matter assumes greater importance in so far as time is not here presented as simple change in the face of the immutability of the sacred, but is considered to be plastic, variously representable like space. And indeed, Hubert harks back to a review of the preceding year when he affirmed: "Time is an object of collective representations in the same way as space".[43] In fact, what is at stake in the end is nothing less than a sociology of time. For a better understanding of this accumulation of the objectives, we must read the article in three different ways. The first reading will reveal the articulations of rites and of a modified time capable of accommodating them; and the second will disclose a theory of religious time; the third will bring to light the principles of a sociology of temporal representation.

To begin with, it is easy to establish the narrow connexion between rites and time, and that on two counts. On the one hand rites usually call for a periodicity; on the other, they are generally situated in time: "the rite always retains a minimum of temporal determination which relates it to the occasion that gives rise to it".[44] It will be noted that from the outset Hubert refers to two distinct aspects of time, which we shall need to come back to later: time as the fulcrum of intervals and time as a set of reference points enabling an event to be positioned. In one respect, their reference to myths sets them outside time — therein lies the paradox — but note the tendency to temporalise the myth. It is situated at the beginning or at the end of a period of time. But again, myths are inclined to rejuvenate themselves by assuming the mantle of some dated historic or legendary substitute (the most usual example being the cult of a saint replacing that of a pagan divinity).

This common link with time would only add to the difficulty if we were to admit that the time of the myth —

or the legend, or the tale — is profoundly dissimilar from ours. A hero can have remained away from home for thirty years in successive sojourns whose total length is very much less.[45] Can it not be said that mythical time, like that of the rite, is periodic? That would already be a large step in bringing them closer together. In Hubert's eyes it is not enough. He tries to demonstrate that there is a "time-environment"[46] where both are situated.

These properties can be reduced to five in number: critical dates interrupt the continuity of time; intervals bounded by two associated critical dates are, in themselves, continuous and indivisible; critical dates are equivalent to the intervals they limit; similar parts are equivalent; some quantitatively unequal durations are equalised and vice versa.[47]

Rather than examine these properties one by one, which would imply their independence,[48] we must try to see their systematic unity. To begin with, from a negative point of view, the properties conflict term by term with those of mathematical time. Hubert had read Bergson and quotes him: magico-religious time bears the same relationship to secular time as mathematical time does to the duration.[49]

What we have then is quality rather than quantity, discontinuity rather than continuity, indivisibility rather than the capability of infinite subdivision, interpenetration rather than exteriority, properties which, as Bergson remarked, are properties of space.

But whilst Bergson destructures time in order to make the duration the indefinitely varied and fluid course of the consciousness,[50] Hubert makes of the properties of this time-environment a framework structured by rules of operation which enable the rite to function. One can prove — and Hubert does prove with examples — that each of these properties structures mythical evolution like the unfolding of rites and allows communication between them. In sequence, we can take the first three properties as rules of division and the last two as rules of equivalence. We shall see that the former are ordered with the latter. The rules of division can indeed be subsumed into a common perspective, that of compact temporal units where the critical date indicates the content as well as the moment. The most characteristic example, in this respect, is the festival. Hence the obvious fact, in a sense, that the critical date interrupts the continuity of time, a fact less obvious when the date comes to marking the inauguration of a different time. Hence also the indivisibility without which the moment would lose all significance, but which does not exclude the division into parts (the successive acts of the festival). Hence finally the third property which does not initially appear to add anything to the first two and whose import Hubert makes clear: "whenever a phenomenon or an appropriate action occurs at any moment in the period which is conventionally assigned to it, it is considered to fill it with its qualities, pervading it entirely".[51]

Equivalences, in keeping with their nature, can appear to be simple rules of measurement. That is certainly the significance of the fifth property. But as a corollary to the preceding one, it can also be considered a prerequisite. Admittedly our temporal equalities must be set aside if we wish to proceed further, that is to say, towards new equivalences based this time on similarity:

> Symmetrical parts of time, that is, those which occupy the same position in the calendar, can be defined as similar among themselves, just like the durations of different length which are taken in turn as units of time. The week, the month, the season, the year, the

cycle of years are presented, in certain cases, as similar among themselves.[52]

One can see that similarity is understood to have a meaning closely akin to the one it has in geometry: we could speak of geometrical similarity.[53] However, there is more to it than correspondences. From equivalence Hubert moves on to identity. It is the foundation of repetition in the myth as well as in the rite: "Every year, every seven years, every nine years, on the same date as the original catastrophe, the town revives, the bells ring, the lady of the chateau leaves her seclusion, the treasury is opened, the custodians go to sleep".[54] It is according to the same principle that the same festivals recur on the same dates. It is because in religious time, and in a wholly general way, "the same dates bring back the same event". It is obvious how fundamental all this is when we now bring together the mythical fact and the rite that is articulated with it. From equivalence, we pass to replication. The Christian Easter perpetuates the Jewish Passover and Paschal sacrifice, as well as the sacrifice of Calvary and the resurrection of Christ. By that we mean that they are replicated, they are renewed. And if Easter Sunday is by tradition the annual date of the resurrection, "the weekly Sunday commemorates the sacrifice of Christ — that is to say, it revives it less solemnly but as effectively as the annual festival of Easter"[55] because of the equivalence relating Sunday to Easter and the week to the year.

It is evident that a second corollary of the rule of equivalence could be that separate moments in secular time can coincide in religious time. Indeed, it gives us the most important rule, establishing a communication between the various parts of this time, in its mythical part and its ritual part. The rules of division then appear to be conditions preventing corresponding parts from taking incompatible forms, like those boxes which can only rest within one another by virtue of all being round or all being square. If we take this view to its logical conclusion, time becomes the equivalent of eternity:

> When all possible equivalences have entered into play, time ends by being represented as a sequence of points which are equivalent to each other and to the intervals which separate them, these intervals themselves being equivalent... In this way, religious and magical actions can cease without being completed, be repeated without changing and be multiplied in time while remaining unique and above time, which is really nothing more than a sequence of eternities.[56]

These characteristics, whose operating powers are manifest, are determined by the penetration into time of what Hubert calls the "category of the sacred". If the first reading of the text focused on its beginning, the second reading offers a more global view — with references to the introduction to the *Manuel d'histoire des religions*[57] — but also prompts a closer look at the central paragraphs.[58]

The essential point is that time itself becomes sacred and not just the beings moving within it. This is necessary to justify the correspondences discussed above. In fact, the "sympathetic associations" — Lévy-Bruhl would say "participation" — between the moments of time of rites and of myths seem to be of the same nature as those which connect sacred objects to each other.

23

> We must expect to see here the idea of magical power, of mana or the sacred, intervene in some way, establishing the belief of which other associations of the same type are the object in magic and religion. The associations which define the qualities of time must have a sacred character, like the terms of which they are composed: in other words, dates or their signs must have magico–religious power, and things signified, events or actions, participate in the nature of this power.[59]

The end of this passage is especially important. On the one hand, the word "participate" is used in it. On the other, dates are presented as "signs". They are, however, sacred signs whose precise characteristic is to participate in the thing which they signify. This sketches the outline of what will become Lévy-Bruhl's theory of the symbol among primitive peoples.[60] Indeed, its nature is to participate and to be also the quality participated in. We have the sacred as category — we shall come to an examination of this term — and the sacred as attribute. This second characteristic is substantiated, materialised almost, in the guise of mana, and identified with the sacred,[61] It is diffused through objects and, in this way, links them together. Thus, whoever receives mana participates in universally widespread mana and thereby participates in the objects and beings receiving that same mana.

This attribute manifests itself in time in two principal ways. First, sacred dates attract one another, come together to the extent of substituting themselves for one another like those of St Martin, St Michael, St Nicholas, Christmas, Twelfth Night, St Anthony, etc.[62] There is an undoubted contradiction between this genuine participation of different times in each other because of their common sacred nature, and the amalgamation of a date with a specific historical or mythical fact. We are then faced with an equilibrium, perpetually called into question, between the specificity of dates and of their tendency to merge and extend their area of fusion. "They are invested with a sort of general qualification which is expressed in particular determinations."[63] Second, it is the characteristic of sacred things to be surrounded by prohibitions. Now the taboo regarding dates is a well-known fact and in conformity with the principles set out above. So too is the taboo regarding the periods which they limit. Hubert seeks to widen the perspective even further: "If we were to follow this reasoning, we would arrive at the notion of an essentially religious time, dangerous and solemn, which would remain unsuited to action if the interdict affecting it as a whole, could not be lifted momentarily and completely distributed among some of its parts."[64]

From there, Hubert returns to the theme of eternity as the limit of sacred time, along with the resonances borrowed from Bergson which we have already encountered.[65]

This notion would be the almost concrete representation of a pure duration, existing in itself and entirely objective, at least as regards human actions, since the rhythm of its passing would not be marked by their succession. Furthermore, this duration, no less inert, immobile and slumbering than man, whose fearful torpor it imprisons, would be a veritable eternity. Here only the necessity to act in order to live, by carving from it successive eternities — shrunken images, yet perfect substitutes for the greatest eternity — would engender time.[66]

So we would come full circle and, from participation to participation, the fixity of the sacred instant would reunite with eternal immobility, rendering the sacralisation of time the means whereby the time in which the rite takes place becomes compatible with sacred eternity.

It is this quasi–logical characteristic of the sacred, an exception to the law of non-contradiction — decidedly, Lévy-Bruhl is my guide here yet again! — which makes it a "category". This is a redoubtable word which, once uttered, gave rise to Henri Berr's criticism[67] and which does not fail to arouse protest if it is taken in its strictly Kantian sense. To make of the sacred a form *a priori* of the understanding is bound to raise difficulties. This is not, however, what Hubert is seeking to do. Certainly, the sacred has universality in common with the Kantian categories — at least, Hubert thinks so, along with all Durkheimians. By this fact, and also because the character of the sacred does not derive from qualities perceived in things, it functions as an *a priori*. But this *a priori* is affective at the same time as it is intellectual.[68] Better still, it marks the flooding of the affective over the intellectual.[69] Mana as a category is the origin of the concept of causality, but it also qualifies this efficient force[70] and bends its conception in a direction determined by our desires, fears and hopes. It can be seen that respect for pure intellect obliged Hubert, like Mauss, to call on the intervention of sentiment to arrive at those "primitive, strange and contradictory forms presented by the notion of time in its relationship with sacred time".[71]

And it is in this way, as a particular time and an abnormal time, that Hubert presents sacred time to begin with, as if a time existed which was simultaneously normal, universal and individual. So we can say, in a sense, that "the notion of the sacred enters as a disturbing element into judgements concerning time".[72] But this is only a manner of speaking: the hypothesis whereby "individuals are provided with a notion of time which each of them separately has abstracted from his or her consciousness"[73] is far from being proved. That is why it is necessary to return to the question of time and its relationship with society in a more general way.

To be sure, Hubert is cautious where the social genesis of the notion of time is concerned. It might be easy to show that religious time has a social origin like everything else that is religious. And it could be just as easy to provide evidence for both the religious and social character of calendars. But what about secular time, that which "functions in our consciousness"? [74] Reasoning by analogy seems to give it an analogous origin. It would then be conceivable that this time, like the other, depends on social rhythms. Hubert is reluctant to take a step which Durkheim[75] — and Halbwachs[76] after him — takes cheerfully. On the other hand, he has no hesitation in asserting the continuity of religious time and our secular time, and the imprint left by the former on the latter.

Now this imprint indicates a sort of conflict inherent in the idea of religious time, but if we look at it from a more general point of view it is the contrast between qualitative and quantitative time. While there might be no need to define the second, the notion of the first is, however, far from being immediately clear. It is precisely on this point that Hubert parts company with Bergson. What are the "differential qualities of the parts of time"? Shall we be able to find them by our intuition of a pure duration? Hubert's reply is plain. "Whether moments or durations, their qualities are defined only by the facts with which they are necessarily and constantly in a positive or negative relation."[77] On the one hand, we find the markers of time, with astronomical phenomena and numbers serving as reference points. On the other, there are events and rites in all their qualitative richness. Time appears at the meeting point of the two series. Then, astronomical reference points become the sign, or to use Hubert's expression the "signature", of qualitative terms. "In themselves, dates are the sign or signature of things that occur on them."[78] Hubert also speaks, a little later on, of the equivalence between "differential qualities of time" and "temporal signatures".

This passage is fundamental to the understanding of social time in Hubert. Indeed, it starts by broadening our perspective. What is in question is no longer merely sacred time, although curiosity might yield a few reminders of it in our current conception of time. It is a genus which encompasses the preceding species and makes up the qualitative time which itself is widespread in our daily social life. Ultimately we are concerned with every calendar. Contrary to the general view, the calendar does not have an essentially quantitative function — and given the current state of affairs, one could scarcely say that its function is mainly religious. "It originates not in the idea of a purely quantitative time, but in that of qualitative time, composed of discontinuous parts, heterogeneous and ceaselessly revolving."[79]

We must hasten to add that this generalisation of qualitative time does not result from a mutation of the intuition of time as the immediate datum of the consciousness. Time, viewed in this way, is a symbolic structure. It appears to be in correspondence with two kinds of phenomena where the one serves as a sign for the other. It is easy to understand the very obvious way in which this symbolic structure, a veritable language — Hubert does not use this

word — falls within the province of culture and is consequently a social phenomenon. Let us pursue this further.
The vocabulary of such a language is of course variable,
each culture having its own dates, times for rites and
festivals. There is even more to it than this, namely, all the
rules which allow the passage from one time to another are
a kind of syntax. We can then readily see that, if Hubert
puts forward the existence of a syntax contrasting secular
and sacred time, the relationship must be broadened and
pluralised. Indeed, we cannot confine ourselves to one
sacred time. Depending on religion, the rules of equivalence will vary — here we see a tendency of the Durkheimian school to make a constant of the sacred. Further,
the passage to a more general notion of qualitative time
permits this pluralisation to be considerably extended.

As we come to the end of this study it is possible to
situate Hubert's outline of a theory of social time within the
collective effort of Durkheim, Hubert and Mauss — the
attempt to formulate a sociological theory of categories.[80]
The problem of the sociology of time is in fact presented by
Hubert and Mauss as correlated with that of the sociology
of space,[81] and together they appear as a specific case of the
sociology of categories which is at the heart of the Durkheimian sociology of knowledge. The question had been
tackled by Durkheim and Mauss in their article on
"Quelques Formes primitives de classification"[82] which
dealt with the social formation of genera. Approaching
categories from this angle evidently owes more to an
Aristotelian than to a Kantian perspective. We should not
therefore be surprised to see categories as the highest
genera, taken as the term of a generalisation of social
experience. Space is regarded essentially as a means of
classification. The division of space into regions is

homologous with the division of living things into species. Now the division into regions echoes the division of society into clans — or more generally into groups. The classification of orientations will follow the same principle. This leads to the principle that it is the structure of society which acts as a model for the structure of space.

This way of seeing things is systematised and emphasised in *The Elementary Forms of Religious Life*. Although Durkheim refers to the Kantian notion of categories, in the end these are only *a priori* in appearance and solely from the point of view of the individual. The ideas which correspond to them are, in fact, the fruit of social experience where society finds its models within itself and then applies them to the rest of the world. Durkheim is very clear on this point:

> Not only has society instituted them [categories], but it is different aspects of the social being which provide their content: to begin with, the category of genus was indistinct from the concept of the human group, it is the rhythm of social life which is the basis for the category of time; it is the space occupied by society which provides the material for the category of space.[83]

We have seen that whereas Hubert participates in this enterprise of sociologising categories, he does not fall into the collective empiricism which consists in somehow reproducing categories in the social organisation presented as a basic datum. Although the idea of social rhythms plays a part in Hubert, his theory of social time is far more sophisticated than a simple record of social rhythms. Time, for Hubert, is a symbolic structure and as this structure is provided with rules, it is also an operating system. It is really a question, as Durkheim wrote, of a time instituted by society but not of a time reproducing aspects of society. The problem of the origin of the idea of time which regularly featured in contemporary philosophies[84] is transcended here because time is taken as an element of the social function itself. This is the significance of the response of Hubert to the question: how does a given society cause its rites to function in relation to the mythical system which is peculiar to them? We can see immediately that by extension, we could ask questions such as, how does a society organise the periodicity of its daily life in accordance with its significant economic and political dates? Or again, how does it organise the rhythm of its political life in accordance with its participation in world history?

4 Conclusion

Some people might draw attention to the originality of Henri Hubert's thought on the subject of popular religion, and some would lay stress on his analysis of the cult of the hero; others again might demonstrate the originality of his sociologising views on prehistory and yet other people would accentuate his picture of Celtic civilization. It is for quite arbitrary reasons that I attach greater importance to Hubert's ideas on time. Such reasons have borne fruit and shown how penetrating the ideas were and how they are capable of further development. Why is it that the "Etude sommaire de la représentation du temps" has been so completely forgotten that contemporary sociological writing on time does not refer to it?

The answer lies in the fact that sociologists have not grasped the social idea of time. Given that it is something particularly elusive, the odds are against establishing the sociology of time. To begin with, it is advisable not to fall into the trap of intuitionalism, that is to say, to avoid rushing in search of time as it is experienced. At the present moment, it must be admitted that we are living in a period when we are intoxicated by speed, permeated with the boredom of lengthy inactivity, and a prey to the anguish of approaching death, but never at any moment do we consider time, or even duration, which are abstractions. From this point of view, time as seen by psychologists appears to be totally artificial, constructed, a function of the experimental mechanisms created to bring it to the fore.[85] But from one extreme to another, we move on to the most abstract notions of time, to the philosophies of time. So we can multiply the perspectives on time in such-and-such a period, and in such-and-such a civilization which are in fact only descriptions of the philosophy of time in those periods or those civilizations. This is certainly an area in which sociology has something to say. But that is how we have missed the essential point, namely, the social reality of time rather than the learned commentaries to which it has given rise.

What Hubert points to is that there is a social organisation of time whose most visible trace is to be found in calendars. Mauss wonders whether Hubert tends to limit himself too closely to festivals.[86] We have seen that Hubert's thought extends further. Moreover, this social organisation goes far beyond a timetable,[87] for that would imply that time is given to us as a kind of table, already drawn up, where we only have to fill in the spaces. Now it is precisely the dimension, the arrangement of the spaces, and in a more subtle way, the possible routes from one to another that are in question. Time appears distinct from phenomena in evolution, when consents and constraints relative to the successions, to the arrests and to the leaps in this evolution, can be demonstrated. Time emerges as an operating medium.

It is there that we discover the most subtle point, one which Hubert had picked out when he wrote at the end of his essay: "In short, the work of abstraction, from which the notion of objective, quantitative and abstract time arose, is perhaps a consequence of the work which separated qualitative and semi–concrete time from things."[88] It is a fact that to be able to talk about this time of social life, we must assume that it is already detached from the events taking place within it. Continuing along this path — the purpose of institutions in the general, Durkheimian sense, like the calendar, the clock, language itself with its names for the parts of time, is to bring about this separation and to establish this duality of time and evolution.[89] It is this duality which someone like Gurvitch failed to recognise in his typology of social times, by piling on top of one another all the variations of rhythm and speed to be found at the heart of social groups.[50] This duality is not, however, a break. Time remains semi–concrete and the stages of evolution remain attached to moments of time by the symbolic adherence that grants time a qualitative aspect giving rise to the variations which are of social origin.

François-André Isambert

NOTES

1. See my article of 1976, "L'Elaboration de la notion de sacré dans l'école durkheimienne", *Archives de sciences sociales des religions*, 42: 35–56.

2. Mauss calls Hubert "my brother worker" several times.

3. It is enough to note that in his foreword to M. Mauss, *Sociologie et anthropologie,* Paris: Presses Universitaires de France, 1950, G. Gurvitch presents the "Essai sur la nature et la fonction du sacrifice" as the work of Mauss, and that in his "Introduction à l'œuvre de Marcel Mauss", at the head of the same work, C. Lévi-Strauss does not mention the contribution of Hubert, despite his co-authorship of the "Esquisse d'une théorie générale de la magie", published in the work. Finally, in his chapter on "Les temps sociaux" in his *La Vocation actuelle de la sociologie,* Paris: Presses Universitaires de France, 1963, Gurvitch does not cite Hubert's article on time, to which, nevertheless, he seems to owe a great deal, at least indirectly.

4. See R. Lantier 1928. This however does not include the two posthumous volumes on the Celts or that on the Germans. (See bibliographies at the end this chapter).

5. A collection of Hubert's works was prepared by Karady and would have followed that of the works of Mauss if material obstacles had not prevented its publication. I am very grateful to Victor Karady for providing me with the dossier he had prepared for this purpose, which supplied me with valuable references.

6. Born on 23 June, 1872, in Paris.

7. As is generally known, *L'Année sociologique* ceased publication just before the war of 1914. A second series, which comprised two volumes, was edited by Mauss (1923–1924 and 1924–1925). The second and final volume appeared

34

in 1927 — by coincidence? — shortly after Hubert's death. The *Annales sociologiques* took over in 1933.

8. 25 May 1927.

9. S. Reinach alludes to a minor disagreement which found them on opposite sides on the occasion of the publication of his *Orpheus*. See Hubert's review in *L'Anthropologie*, 1909: 596.

10. See Hubert 1899a. Although the article appeared in 1899, it was written before the publication of Abbé Duchesne's *Premiers temps de l'Etat pontifical* (1898).

11. This note, for the information of his son, is an intellectual testament allowing the disposal of his manuscripts and expounding the meaning of his works. See Hubert 1979.

12. There is no direct trace of this thesis, which appears never to have been completed. As well as the passage indicated in the "Essai sur la nature et la fonction du sacrifice", a further echo of this work is to be found in the preface to the *Culte du héros* of S. Czarnowski (1919). It is clear that Hubert was especially interested in a demi-god, associated with Hierapolis, and with the goddess, and who in present-day Lebanon takes the name of Eshmoun, or even of Adonis. One might note that a river with reddish water exists to the north of Beirut and is held to be reddened with the blood of Adonis. The "Syrian goddess", sometimes anonymous and sometimes polyonymous, who was celebrated by Lucian, excited the curiosity of a fairly large number of historians at the end of the nineteenth and beginning of the twentieth centuries. It is easy to understand that this divine and polymorphic personality, a link between mythologies, should have interested a mythologist like Hubert.

13. See Hubert 1979.

14. E. Durkheim and M. Mauss, 1903, "De quelques Formes

primitives de classification, contribution à l'étude des représentations collectives", *L'Année sociologique*, VI, 1903: 1–72.

15. See Hubert and Mauss 1906a. It served as a preface to Hubert and Mauss 1909a.

16. M. Mauss, "L'Origine des pouvoirs magiques dans les sociétés australiennes", *Annuaire de l'Ecole Pratique des Hautes Etudes*, Section des Sciences religieuses, 1904: 1–55. Reprinted in Hubert and Mauss 1909a.

17. *L'Année sociologique*, X, 1907: 302–304. In particular: "Not having given this question adequate consideration, we do not know whether these five, or more accurately four, theories cover all the facts. We believe so. But we suspect that the problem of the relationship between the idea of eternity and that of time cannot easily be resolved starting from these facts alone, and yet it is this problem which, in Hubert's own opinion, is of prime importance. We even suspect that his analysis, however complicated it might be, does not actually deal with the conflict which appears to exist between sacred moments and secular duration, between common time, festivals and those dates which seem to arise from substantial and eternal sanctity to divide everyday life into different periods of time. Does Hubert connect this problem with the narrower problem of festivals? We do not know whether he is right or wrong in not doing so here. In any case, it is a mistake not to indicate the reasons for the omission" (ibid.: 304).

18. In 1904, Hubert published a French translation of the *Manuel d'histoire des religions* by Chantepie de la Saussaye, based on the 2nd German edition. See Hubert 1904b. This edition omits the part devoted to religious phenomenology.

19. E. Durkheim, "De la Définition des phénomènes religieux", *L'Année sociologique*, II, 1899: 1–29.

20. Hubert 1904b.

21. Thus Hubert connects the Durkheimian school to German roots, something which Durkheim refused to do in his debate with S. Deploige. See my article of 1976, "L'Elaboration de la notion de sacré dans l'école durkheimienne", *Archives de sciences sociales des religions*, 42: 37, n.7.

22. Including information regarding the place of this particular work of Hubert in Durkheimian thought; see ibid.

23. Hubert 1904b: xxi.

24. Ibid.: xlvii. "Religion is the administration of the sacred".

25. Ibid.

26. S. Czarnowski, *Le Culte des héros et ses conditions sociales. Saint Patrick, héros national de l'Irlande,* Paris: Alcan, 1919.

27. Hubert 1904b: i–iv.

28. Ibid.: xxix.

29. It is here that we recall the case of the companion of the Syrian goddess. It was cited above in relation to Hubert's doctoral thesis, 1904b: xlii and xlvi.

30. "But we still have one mythologist left, it is in fact Granet. There was another, no less penetrating than he, it was Hubert. I am trying to stand in for Hubert and to help Granet" (intervention following a paper by Granet, *Bulletin de l'Institut français de sociologie*, 3, 1933: 112).

31. See Berr 1932b.

32. M. Mauss, "Les Civilisations. Eléments et formes", in *Le*

François-André Isambert

> *mot et l'idée,* 1re Semaine internationale de synthèse, Paris, 1930: 99–100.

33. See Berr 1932a.

34. Ibid.: v.

35. Ibid.

36. Ibid.: vi.

37. The printed publication date is 1932 for both volumes, but the date of the copyright differs by one year.

38. M. Mauss, foreword to Hubert 1932a: xii..

39. Further on, Mauss also wrote: "We hope to publish elsewhere, in another volume under the name of Henri Hubert, an unabridged version of the course in sociology describing the Celts. This only gives a basic impression of it."

40. See the synoptic table of the state of completion of the lectures on both texts, by P. Chalus, in his foreword to Hubert 1952.

41. This former pupil was probably O. Janse. (See Mauss's foreword to Hubert 1932a: xx.n.1). His work, along with Hubert's manuscript, served as the basis for Mauss's course at the Collège de France on the formation of the Germanic civilisations, 1933–1940. See V. Karady (ed.), *Marcel Mauss, Œuvres,* Paris: Editions de Minuit, 1968, II: 574).

42. H. Hubert, Introduction to the section on ritual, *L'Année sociologique*, V, 1902: 247–8.

43. *L'Année sociologique*, IV, 1901: 234, the opening sentence of the review of the book by W. W. Fowler, *The Roman*

Festivals of the Period of the Republic.

44. Hubert [1905] 1909a:191.

45. Ibid.: 196.

46. Ibid.: 194–195.

47. According to the list of contents in 1909: 235.

48. In his review, Mauss reduces these properties to four, making the last one the corollary of the preceding one.

49. Hubert [1905] 1909a: 210.

50. See the penetrating analysis by V. Jankélévitch, *Bergson*, Paris: Alcan, 1931.

51. Hubert [1905] 1909a: 202.

52. Ibid.: 204–205.

53. On the other hand, Hubert is less happy in his choice of the word "symmetrical", whose meaning would surely be better conveyed by the word "homologous".

54. Ibid.: 205.

55. Ibid.: 206.

56. Ibid.: 206–207. Doubtless a Bergsonian resonance. A little further on, p.210, Hubert refers to *Matière et mémoire* and to the idea of memory as a tension of the consciousness between the moments of the duration, a tension which, in Bergson, accepts eternity as a limiting case, as the sum total of the entire duration.

57. See Hubert 1904b.

58. Hubert [1905] 1909a: 219–224.

59. Ibid.: 220.

60. See *L'Expérience mystique et les symboles chez les primitifs*, Paris: Alcan, 1938

61. For the identification of *mana* and the sacred, see n.1 above.

62. Hubert [1905] 1909a: 221.

63. Ibid.: 220.

64. Ibid.: 222.

65. See *Matière et mémoire*, pp.231–232.

66. Hubert [1905] 1909a: 222.

67. Berr 1906: 16.

68. Here once more, we call to mind Lévy-Bruhl and his "affective category of the supernatural", see *L'Expérience mystique et les symboles chez les primitifs*, Paris: Alcan, 1938.

69. See preface to Hubert and Mauss 1909: xxvi–xxvii.

70. Durkheim will write in *Les Formes élémentaires de la vie religieuse*, Paris: Alcan, 1912: 628: "It is the collective force which was the prototype for the concept of efficacious force, an essential element of the category of causality."

71. Hubert and Mauss: xxxi.

72. Hubert [1905] 1909a: 224.

73. Ibid.: 226.

74. Ibid.: 227.

75. See n.70 above: 630.

76. *Les Cadres sociaux de la mémoire*, Paris, Alcan, 1925; *Mémoire et société*, Paris, Presses Universitaires de France, 1950.

77. Hubert [1905] 1909a: 211.

78. Ibid.

79. Ibid.: 229.

80. See the article by H. Berr. Mauss often refers to this group of three associated with the sociology of knowledge.

81. Hubert 1904b: xx.

82. *L'Année sociologique*, VI: 1–72.

83. *Les Formes élémentaires*: 628. See n.70 above.

84. The best known and most discussed book at that time, which itself discussed the views of Wundt and of Ribot, is J.-M. Guyau, *La genèse de l'idée de temps*, Paris: Alcan, 1890.

85. See for example the analysis — incidentally, an outstanding one — of P. Fraisse in his *Psychologie du temps*, Paris: Presses Universitaires de France, 1957.

86. See the critique in n.17 above.

87. A book like that of W. Grossin, *Les Temps de la vie quotidienne*, Paris: Mouton, 1974, does not go beyond this level of analysis. That was not, however, its objective.

88. Hubert [1905] 1909a: 229.

89. Which J.-M. Guyau believed could be set in the absolute by means of the metaphorical contrast between the *course* of the river of time and its *bed*.

90. See Gurvitch, *La Multiplicité des temps sociaux*, Paris, Cours Documentation Université (Sorbonne), 1961, reprinted in *Vocation actuelle de la sociologie*; see n.3 above.

ESSAY ON TIME

A brief study of the representation of time in religion and magic*

Henri Hubert

The problem that forms the object of this study was posed in Volume V of the *Année sociologique*.[1] There it was assumed that the acts and representations of religion and, it might be added, of magic entail ideas of time and space that are quite different from the usual ones. Given, it was said, that rites and mythical events take place in space and time, it is necessary to ask how the theoretical separation of time and space can be reconciled with the infinitude and immutability of the "sacred", in which rites and mythical events take place too. In order to simplify our vocabulary, I will widen the meaning of the word "sacred" as much as possible, understanding by it both the religious sacred and the magical sacred, the sacred proper and *mana*, even though we have already distinguished between them elsewhere.[2] Hypothetically, it has been assumed up to now that while the sacred, without distinction of type, may be susceptible to endless limitations, it is theoretically indivisible, and that as soon as it manifests itself, it does so entirely.[3] This is how its actual presence in the sacrifice was explained, as well as the undefined properties of magical things and acts.

* Translated by Robert Parkin and Jacqueline Redding from H. Hubert, "Etude sommaire de la représentation du temps dans la religion et la magie", *Annuaire de l'Ecole Pratique des Hautes Etudes, Section des Sciences Religieuses*, 1905: 1-39.

Having proposed that we study what is known of the primitive divisions of the year among the ancient Germanic nations during this year's course, I have tried to group the anomalies generally presented by the calculation of time in religion by way of a preface. These anomalies, which betray the contradiction between the respective characteristics of normal time and the sacred, are such as to put us on the track of the notion of religious time. I shall take it as established that this religious notion of time is the one which has presided over the development of calendars. There is no need to prove further that calendars were actually created in a religious context.

Besides, they involve a confused network of details, in the distinction and determination of dates and periods, which neither the observation of concrete durations nor the abstract idea we have of time — that is to say, the idea of a continuous span, indefinitely divisible into successive parts, homogeneous and impenetrable — is sufficient to account for. It is the gist of these lectures that I propose to give here.

In this study, I will not be concerned with psychology nor, therefore, with describing the variable judgements of different individuals concerning durations, nor with explaining the incoherence of these judgements. The representations on which my study bears have something of the conceptual and also of the conventional about them. They are universal in collectivities and have a sort of legislative rigidity. Nor do I aspire to push the analysis of the idea of time towards the metaphysical. I am simply seeking to know what this idea actually has been, and that only in respect of certain classes of judgements and lines of argument which, up to a certain point, concern religion and magic.

The very plan of my course has imposed upon me the choice of facts upon which my conclusions are based. I have abridged the exposition as much as possible, so as to remain within the confines of this study. The Greek and Roman religions and Christianity have provided examples and points of comparison. Naturally, in the first instance I was motivated to concern myself with the facts emerging from these religions by reason of the historical connections that exist between them and those of the Germans. There will be occasion to carry these researches further, especially into the various domains of ethnography.

1

Let us propose as a principle that time is a necessary condition of magical and religious acts and representations. Attention has already been drawn on many occasions to the fact that rites are carried out in conditions of time, which are constant for the same rite and which contribute to the definition of their specific environment.[4] Periodic rites are, by definition, associated with fixed dates of the calendar or with the regular recurrence of certain phenomena. Occasional rites are also carried out at determined moments. Many of them give rise to the predictions of horoscopes, which are sometimes complicated beyond the bounds of probability. Such requirements may well be reduced to the last extremity, but the rite always retains a minimum of temporal determination which relates it to the occasion that gives rise to it. The examination of any ritual will suffice to show that rites vary by reason of the circumstances of time, if not in their essential structure, at least in their accompanying details and in the preparations and attitude they call for.

It is true that mythical events seem to take place outside of time or — what comes to the same thing — within the total extent of time, since, as their repetition in rituals shows in particular, they succeed in being equally contemporary to dates spaced out in normal time. However, all mythologies attempt to situate this eternity in a chronological series, generally at the start of time, sometimes at the end. It is for this reason that myths, whatever else they may be, are either origin myths or eschatological myths: they account for the origin or end of things, not because this is essentially their function as myths, but because they exist in time. Moreover, they are fixed indiscriminately in one place or the other and are differentiated only secondarily from this point of view: in fact, as has been rightly noted, myths of origin and myths of the end of the world have elements in common.[5] A consequence of this is that myths everywhere tend to be systematised in the form of traditions relating to the origins of the societies that produce them. Bodies of myths constitute a prehistory of humanity, of the tribe or nation; the gods are the source of human families. The synthesis of the diverse currents of religious representations takes this form not because myths in general arise from the divinisation of ancestors, but because they are imagined within time. It is for the same reason that rites are generally presented as commemorating the myths which are attached to them, reproducing indefinitely an event which is supposed to have taken place at one point in time, on a fixed date.

But is not situating myths at the origin of time, in the mists of time, just a crude and simple way of indicating their eternity? This would be the case, were it not for another phenomenon that occurs just as frequently, namely the rejuvenation of myths. We have examples of this in festivals associated with several myths or whose institution is successively bound up with different causes and dates, spread out in time. In Rome, the Poplifugia commemorated in turn the flight of the people at the death of Romulus, another flight of Romans during a war against the Fidenates, and finally, after 42 BC, by virtue of a *senatus consultum*, the birthday, perhaps conventional, of Julius Caesar.[6] In Christian Europe, the patron saints of parish festivals have often been rejuvenated: a younger saint is placed alongside, or sometimes replaces, a time–worn one. This is how, for example, the cult of Francis of Paulus became widespread in Sicily and Provence.[7] At Lezoux (Puy–de–Dôme), the patron saint of the parish is giving way to a Jesuit of the same name martyred in China fifty years ago. The ritual combats of popular festivals become dramatic representations of historical combats, memories of the Arab and Norman invasions of Sicily, of the English and Arab invasions of France.[8] Many festivals which are presented as the anniversaries of the founding of parish churches seem to be ancient agrarian festivals with complex functions. Instead of commemorating a mythical fact, going back to the beginning of time, they commemorate a historical fact. Moreover, the rejuvenated myth always becomes the point of departure for the periodic celebration of the rite, since either the memory of previous periods is obliterated, or else a new and more efficacious consecration of the chosen date is imagined. Examples of this phenomenon are just as abundant outside the history of festivals. In Wales, the semi–historical figure of Arthur was substituted for that of some god slumbering in mountain caves,[9] just as, similarly, Frederick Barbarossa replaced certain mythical figures.[10]

Thus myths are rejuvenated in history, drawing on elements of reality which consolidate the belief of which they are the object as myths. But this is not because mythical truth is poorly distinguished for believers from the historical truth that the myths embody; it is because they need to be situated in time with a precision that must increase with the growing precision of the representation of things in time. The rejuvenation of myths is not a different phenomenon from the general phenomenon of their localisation in the past, but a particular form of the same phenomenon.

But that is not all. Magical or religious events, whether rites or images, are not simply conceived of as happening before, after or during other events: they are situated in a time-environment that is relatively abstract and detached from things that endure. In truth, the image of the latter is still mixed up with the idea of the former. A semi–concrete representation, this image retains the memory of real durations. To begin with, the rhythm of ideal time may be indicated by certain of these durations. But it not only dominates them, it imposes theoretical and practical limits on them all. The idea of this-time environment enters as a distinct element into the speculations of magic and religion.

Time is usually represented as a system of dates and successive durations, a system which periodically repro-duces itself and whose different lengths are supposedly equal in series and symmetrical from period to period. The notation of the points and intervals within a limited and repeatable period constitutes the calendar.

Is the calendar a system of measuring time for religion and magic? Are religious or magical acts divided in the same way as the acts of our civic life appear to be divided?

Have religion and magic found convenient points of reference for carrying out actions which must be repeated in a system elaborated for other ends? I do not think so. In fact, there exist calendrical systems devised especially to regulate the periodicity of religious or magical acts, systems which are or have been employed for this particular purpose in parallel with the usual calendars. Such is the *tonalamatl* of 260 days which, among the Aztecs, ran parallel to the solar year, and the weekly calendar which among ourselves serves to establish the date of Easter, a calendar which has itself become the model for the civic calendar in Iceland.[11] The existence of these systems attests to the need for a specific rhythm which governs the dispersal of religious acts in time. For religion and magic, the object of a calendar is not to measure time, but to endow it with rhythm.

Thus on the one hand, rites are necessarily distributed in a time divided by fixed, regularly spaced points. On the other hand, religious representations, besides assigning limits to divine eternities and allowing gods to die, also assume the time in which durations of every type elapse, especially divine ones, to have a rhythm. The different millenarianisms — those of Judeo–Christianity, Zoroastrianism, the Hindu *kalpa* system — are proof of this. Our fairy tales, especially those which involve kidnappings, lead one to think that spirits periodically pass by the same places; it is then that spells cast earlier are lifted. Princesses in lost castles can be freed from a magic spell at a magic moment which occurs at intervals. In sum, mythic eternities are periodic.[12]

This is not to say that they have a measure, let alone a measure in common with normal time. Comparisons reveal a profound difference. Especially in tales, the calculation of time presents an unbelievable incoherence. A Macedonian story-teller assures us, without turning a hair, that a hero who took three years to descend to the Antipodes and twelve years to climb back up again, without spending an appreciable length of time down there, remained thirty years outside his own country.[13] The contradiction does not shock him, for it is a fairytale, αὐτο 'ναι παραμύθι.

It is with the help of similar contradictions that the antinomy between divisible time and the indivisible sacred, which seeds itself within time, are reconciled. However, it might be thought that these syntheses are achieved by simply fiddling with the quantitative rigour of the common notion of time. I do not think so. On the contrary, I believe they denote the existence of another idea, whose constant and definable characteristics are approximately those I am going to describe.

2

Considering in turn the differentiated elements in the representation of time — that is, critical dates and intervals — I will put forward a certain number of propositions relative to their intrinsic properties or reciprocal relations which will serve us in characterising the notion as a whole. I will not set out these propositions as absolutes, or waste effort looking for detracting exceptions. I do not claim that the idea of time in religion and magic always differs from the common idea of time: it is enough for it to differ from it frequently and for the differences involved to be regular. An examination of them will show that, for magic and religion, *the successive parts of time are not homogeneous*, that the parts which appear to us as equal in length are not necessarily equal, nor even equivalent: *parts considered similar are homogeneous and equivalent* by reason of their place in the calendar. From this, it follows that such an idea of time is not one of pure quantity but is more complex than that which corresponds to it in the ordinary course of our mental life. It is not possible to study it in the abstract: the properties of the parts of time are deduced from their relations with the concrete durations that they frame.

Let me add, for greater clarity, that I am not only concerned in this study with the divisions of the calendar. By critical dates are understood not only the extreme limits of sections of the calendar, but also every moment which is the object of special consideration. The cycle of calendrical terms is only one of the particular systems of critical dates and intervals that revolve in time.

1 Critical dates interrupt the continuity of time

This can be proved by showing that they break up particular durations. A society which divides time into durations, whose length is expressed as a number of days, months or years — seven or nine, for example[14] — imposes the same rhythmic divisions on durations, which have no other reason to be thus limited and divided than the law stated above.

If the durations in question did not actually end on the critical date, their actual interruption was sometimes formally expressed in rites. In Sparta, the kings were sub-mitted to an ordeal every nine years. The Ephors assembled on the night of a full moon and observed the sky: if a shooting star crossed it, the king, suspected of some religious transgression, was provisionally deposed until the

Oracle at Delphi had pronounced on his case.[15] This nine–
yearly rhythm, to which the power of the kings of Sparta
was thus subjected, appears to have been general in the
sphere of Cretan civilization. Tradition has it that Minos
was also obliged to present himself every nine years at
the cave on Mount Ida to have his royal authority
renewed.[16]

This is just one example among an infinitude of possible
examples, for the phenomenon is general. When magistracies terminated at the end of the year, annual or cyclical
fires had to be extinguished, vessels or clothes renewed,
provisions entirely consumed or destroyed, before pro-
ceeding to the series of representations. I have chosen the
example deliberately because in this case the critical date is
not a festival in the true sense of the word, one which might
in itself imply such consequences, but simply the ending of
a period whose observation does not even appear to be
determined by the dominant chronological system. This
shows that the critical dates of the time-environment break
up concrete durations — which, in themselves, are independent of them — out of a kind of necessity; they break
up the abstract duration of which they form a part all the
more. They are truly critical and dangerous: for doctors in
antiquity, illnesses and human life in general were tied,
untied and retied at periodic intervals of seven days, seven
months or seven years.[17] In short, the time in which magical
and religious events take place is discontinuous: it
progresses by fits and starts. That is not all. We can already
see that the parts we distinguish are not homogeneous.
Indeed, the moment which constitutes the critical date
necessarily differs from whichever moment of the durations
precedes or follows it. On the other hand, durations
separated by critical dates differ amongst themselves, since

acts or events begin or cease by the very fact of their appearance.

2 Intervals bounded by two associated critical dates are, in themselves, continuous and indivisible

A first indication of the continuity of these intervals is provided by rites of entry and exit, of which they are often the object. These rites, comparable to those marking the beginning and end of religious ceremonies, give such intervals the appearance of a continuous whole, all of whose parts are solidary, like those of a sacrifice. The Roman year opened at the calends of March by taking the auspices; it was brought to an end in January and February with a series of inauspicious days and expiatory ceremonies.[18] The most remarkable and significant form of these rites is to be found in those cases — of which European folklore offers a great number — in which the year or season that is beginning or ending is personified, so that it can be dramatically ushered in or expelled.[19] Here, the individuality of the parts of time even acquires personality. As already mentioned, the extinction and lighting of fires with the passage from one period to another are rites of entry and exit comparable with the preceding ones. Moreover, these rites are or may be simultaneously valid for the durations themselves and for what takes place within them: the fire that usage has profaned is extinguished, the transgressions committed during the year are expelled, the work of the season is inaugurated. It would take too long to demonstrate that this confusion should not concern us for the moment. In effect, abstract and concrete durations are identified with one other.

What is more, ideal associations are established between various sorts of periods and things that endure, associations in which the period–form is the unit of time in the duration–substance. This observation allows us to proceed a step further.

Not only is there an attempt to equalise the duration of events and things with the duration of periods of time, to inaugurate acts at the beginning of them,[20] but also to avoid or prohibit the undertaking of certain serious enterprises — a war, for example — in the course of a period. There are some famous examples of this, such as Ariovistus post-poning active hostilities until the new moon,[21] the Spartans waiting for the full moon before taking the field,[22] and the Athenians waiting until the seventh day of the month.[23]

These prohibitions show the preoccupation with endowing the time in which rites take place with a spasmodic character, which inevitably results from the succession of points of rest described above and from their indivisible intervals. In their fear of upsetting the order of things with an untoward initiative, men burden themselves with rules for preserving — in so far as it depends on them — this same necessary order, which their beliefs show them to be perfectly realised in the world. This is actually a generally established idea, one which governs experience as well as disturbing it and out of which our ancestors have made a truly scientific law, namely that if certain phenomena commence at the start of a certain period they last the whole of the period, and that they wait for the start of a period before beginning. Meteorological sayings are a rather good example of these pseudo-scientific traditions.[24]

Thus, if we acknowledge the establishment of a formal association between the duration of certain concrete things and certain periods of abstract time, considered as their measure, as their unit of time, we can see that these periods are either completely filled up with the durations in question or else exclude them entirely. The length of the concrete durations is entirely comparable with that of the corresponding periods. In order to explain this, we can always resort to the hypothesis of a magico–religious necessity arbitrarily determining the length of the durations. But also, we can explain this very necessity if we assume, as already stated, that the different units of time are conceived of as indivisible, for in this case the period–form will coincide completely with the duration-substance of which it is the rhythmic measure. There are, in fact, two measures which cannot be divided into smaller lengths in relation to each other. In prohibiting the undertaking of certain acts except at the start of the corresponding periods, ritual is simply trying to bring the activities of men into conformity with their habits of thought. It goes without saying that the periods can only be represented as indivisible if taken separately and each by itself, or solely in their relation to the events which are deemed to be of a nature to fill them entirely. Each interval of critical dates is, in effect, divided into shorter intervals by other critical dates. From this point of view, durations can be compared with numbers, which are considered in turn as the enumeration of inferior units or as sums capable of serving as units for the composition of superior numbers. They are given continuity by the mental operation which synthesises their elements. I accept that a similar mental synthesis embraces at a stroke the length of period–forms and of duration–substances.

This reservation having been made, I conclude first, that parts of time are conceived of as not being indefinitely divisible into successive parts, and secondly, that each subdivision is constant in relation to itself and heterogeneous in relation to the subdivisions of the same series which precede and follow it.

3 Critical dates are equivalent to the intervals they limit

We may deduce from the preceding proposition that, whenever a phenomenon or an appropriate action occurs at any moment in the period which is conventionally assigned to it, it is considered to fill it with its qualities, pervading it entirely. The prohibitions cited above against embarking on a series of important actions, like war, once a period has begun allow us to draw this conclusion: by virtue of this fatal contamination, the clash of contradictory actions in the same time period is to be feared no less acutely than the rupture of its continuity.

What is probable for any moment of a duration can be no less probable for the characteristic moments of this duration. The presumption here is all the stronger in that the critical points which define the said duration constitute essential elements of its representation. In fact, at the start of the ritual period, prophylactic rites,[25] vows,[26] blessings[27] and sympathetic rites valid for the whole period[28] are carried out. In another connection, the phenomena taking place at this decisive hour give predictions for the duration which they inaugurate.[29] The beginning entails what follows: what must occur throughout the entire extent of this duration is implicit from the outset, at least in representation, and vice versa. The belief in the persistence for a definite time of the effects produced at a given moment is the principle behind the displacement of some rites and the concentration of those which can be repeated indefinitely on chosen dates. Consequently, this belief holds an important place in representations of magic and religion. In short, they are indifferent to whether the rite is completed at the beginning of a duration or throughout its length. The critical date and the period that follows it are assimilated. In other words, they are homogeneous and, their dimensions apart, liable to be regarded as equivalents.

The reason for this assimilation is the one I gave above. No measurement is possible between the event in question and the period with which it is mentally associated, nor between the instant in which it takes place and the period of which this instant is a part. They are neither comparable extents, nor antithetical elements; moment and duration, event and duration, are identified in the same mental operation, which is absolutely synthetic. Proof of this perfect assimilation of critical dates and their intervals is furnished by the very names of the time which originally and properly designated the critical dates.[30] Intervals and instants converge.

One objection remains to be eliminated, namely, that the effects and phenomena in question, being conceived of as durable, necessarily last beyond the moment at which they began. But that need not be an obstacle. The essential thing is that they only last the time of a definite period, all of whose moments, in conformity with my second proposition, constitute an indistinct whole, and that they end exactly on one of these critical dates, which, in conformity with my first proposition, interrupt this continuity.

We must therefore enter a new conclusion, which is that not only are durations not conceived as indefinitely divisible into distinct and homogeneous parts, but that these parts are interpenetrable.

4 Similar parts are equivalent

Symmetrical parts of time, that is, those which occupy the same position in the calendar, can be defined as similar among themselves, just like the durations of different length which are taken in turn as units of time: the week, the month, the season, the year, the cycle of years are presented, in certain cases, as similar among themselves.

The first point is that critical dates and the intervals they limit, whose homogeneity and equivalence we have just demonstrated and which occupy the same relative position in the calendar, are similar. For the rest, the equivalence of similar parts is demonstrated by the fact that chronological similarity entails or permits the repetition of the same events. The same representations are attached to them, of a sort that appear to be exact reproductions of each other: they are conducive to identity. In legends of castles, towns, monasteries or submerged churches, the curse is never definitive but is renewed periodically. Every year, every seven years, every nine years, on the same date as the original catastrophe, the town revives, the bells ring, the lady of the chateau leaves her seclusion, the treasury is opened, the guardians go to sleep; but at the appointed hour, the charm regains its power and everything falls back under its spell. These periodic lapses are almost sufficient to show that the same dates bring back the same events. The whole of astrology and part of ancient and popular science are founded on this principle. Conversely, the same religious or magical acts are completed in the same circumstances of time, that is, at certain symmetrical points of any system of dividing time, be it a standard calendar or a special one, astronomical or other. This is enough to prove the care employed in indicating for each rite the temporal conditions of a complete ritual. Ultimately, the same festivals are celebrated on the same dates.

But there are degrees of similarity, and the more important the rite the greater the resemblance. The intensity of attention given to this resemblance in certain cases reveals the importance attached to it and the efficacy it is supposed to have. Thus the determination of the date of Easter was one of the central preoccupations of early Christianity. The Christian Easter, which perpetuated the Jewish Passover and the Paschal sacrifice on the one hand and the sacrifice of Calvary and the resurrection of Christ on the other, had to be celebrated at exactly the same point in time as the events it reproduced, that is to say, at a point exactly symmetrical with that at which they were first produced — a delicate problem, since it was necessary to find these symmetrical points in two different calendars, whose different discrepancies could not be calculated exactly. Infinite scruple was brought to bear on the choice of an approximate solution.[31]

The weekly Sunday commemorates the sacrifice of Christ — that is to say, it revives it less solemnly but as effectively as the annual festival of Easter. And what Sunday is to Easter, the week is to the year and, in so far as the year represents the entire course of time, the week stands for it too.[32] In India, the first twelve days of the month were equivalent to the twelve months that followed; indeed, a continuous sacrifice, extending throughout these twelve days, was equivalent to a similar sacrifice lasting the entire year and was valid for that same year.[33]

When all possible equivalences have entered into play, time ends by being represented as a sequence of points which are equivalent to each other and to the intervals which separate them, these intervals themselves being equivalent; and as a sequence of parts of unequal length, nested within one another and equivalent in the same way, each point and each period standing respectively for the whole. In this way, religious and magical actions can cease without being completed, be repeated without changing and be multiplied in time while remaining unique and above time, which is really nothing more than a sequence of eternities.

5 Some quantitatively unequal durations are equalised and vice versa

The expression of indeterminate durations through precise numbers — 7, 9, 50, etc. — is a constant and well-known fact, of which it would be superfluous to give examples. When employed in this way, conventional numbers correspond to the exact length of periods determined by certain current or obsolete systems of dividing time:[34] weeks of seven or nine days, divisions of the month or lunar month, have been the typical example of periods of seven and nine days, or seven and nine years, whose length is obviously conventional. Fixed and indefinite lengths are represented as equal. On the other hand, it is a commonplace of mythology and folklore — one which has its counterpart in our individual experience — that, according to circumstance, durations do not elapse at the same speed, for this changes with the passage from the supernatural to the normal life of men.[35] A shepherd who falls asleep for an hour wakes up after a hundred years; returning from a visit to the fairies, he finds only new generations in his village. Conversely, heroes can live years of magical life in a single hour of human life. Time counts no more than space in their course through the world. The numerically corresponding parts of the Hindu *kalpa*s are not conceived as being of the same length.[36]

3

It does not follow from these facts that time is not a quantity for magic and religion or capable of being considered as such, but that it is not a pure quantity, homogeneous in all its parts, always comparable with itself and exactly measurable. Something other than considerations of more, less and the same enter into judgements which bear on time: there are also considerations of suitability, opportunity, continuity, constancy and similarity, and the equivalences of which we have spoken are not equalities. Units of time are not units of measurement but of a rhythm where oscillation between alternatives periodically leads back to the similar.

Subdivisions of time are not lengths defined solely by their dimension and relative position. Other elements, which explain their quantitative anomalies, enter into the notion, such as the idea of active qualities whose presence renders them homogeneous or heterogeneous in relation to one another. If a certain quality enters into the representation of each section of time, this will naturally be conceived of as being equally distributed in all its parts: if one thinks of it solely in respect of this quality, each period will necessarily be homogeneous in relation to itself. The homogeneity of time will cease at the end of each period, the following period bringing with it new differential qualities. Similar parts will be equivalent and homogeneous or rather identical, because they will have the same quality. Finally, the relative value of durations will not just depend on their absolute extent but also on the nature and intensity of their qualities.

In brief, the propositions enumerated above cease to be contradictory as soon as one ceases to consider time as an environment without qualities. Furthermore, it is not a pure concept, a sort of geometric locus distinguished by abstraction from the mass of particular durations, but a sort of entity which is potent in the same way as a magical act, existing objectively and distinct from successive and lasting phenomena, since it divides them up in its own way. Its divisions are not simply ideal but real and effective, since they brutally interrupt the substance they frame.

In truth, the qualities I have spoken of are those of parts of time. It is reasonable to ask whether the idea of time in general does not entail similar qualities, and even whether the particularities which distinguish the parts are anything more than the diverse modalities of a common quality of time. However, it is difficult to perceive at first what might be the qualities of this religious and magical time. Perhaps it has, on the whole, only a natural disposition for receiving qualities. For the moment, however, it is sufficient to bring to light the qualitative nature attributed to time in general by noting the qualities recognised in its parts. These are very obvious, and they become evident in being contrasted with one another. The parts of time are not indifferent to the things that might happen within them and either attract or exclude them — whence, on the one hand, an inexhaustible series of predictions founded solely on the distinction of dates, and on the other, a series of positive or negative prescriptions relative to days,[37] the most typical of which are the negative prescriptions otherwise known as taboos of time. What has just been said of days is also valid for periods. Months, for example, have a constant qualitative content in relation to one another, which gives them a genuine individuality.[38] If need be, their place in the solar year and the diversity of the operations, agricultural or otherwise, which, in the nature of things, are carried out in them can be taken as the principle of their differentiation. But remove this, and there still remains a residue of differential prescriptions, such as, among others, the prohibition of marriage in the month of May, in which are revealed the qualities peculiar to them. I therefore accept provisionally that the parts of time and time in general are conceived of as being endowed with or capable of having qualities.

4

Here, my investigation parallels philosophical analyses which have recently made the representation of the duration in the individual consciousness their object. In his *Données immédiates de la conscience*,[39] Bergson has come to the conclusion that the notion of time does not only involve that of quantity, but that it is also qualitative. In the subtle arabesques of his *Matière et mémoire*,[40] he replaces ideas of length, position and succession as the generating element of the representation of time with the idea of an active tension through which, on the one hand, the harmony of independent durations of different rhythms is realised in the consciousness, and on the other, images are distributed and circulated among the different planes of this same consciousness. In his system, this is how the idea of time is transferred from the domain of pure quantity to that of quality.

We shall come even closer to the theory of time as a scale of tensions in the consciousness if we are more precise in our attempt to take account of the qualities which constitute the notion of time for magic and religion. In order to study this from the most accessible point of view, let us provisionally consider only the differential qualities of the parts of time. Whether moments or durations, their qualities are defined only by the facts with which they are necessarily and constantly in a positive or negative relation. On the one hand there are natural phenomena, astronomical or otherwise, which are chosen as markers of time, or numbers, which express the theoretical length of periods;[41] on the other hand there are representations, which the recurrence of the first terms necessarily entails or repels, and actions, which are carried out or evaded in order to realise, as far as is possible, the associations believed to be necessary. The elements thus associated are intimately united and entail one another, the one lasting as long as the second.[42] This system of relations is properly speaking a system of signatures. In themselves, dates are the sign or signature of things that occur on them,[43] in the same way that a planetary conjunction is the signature of such and such an event or such and such a rite. Thus differential qualities of time and temporal signatures are equivalent expressions. To begin with, therefore, when trying to imagine what might be the qualitative elements of the representation of time in magic and religion, one only encounters associated images, whose association is retained in view of possible actions.

This first conclusion agrees with Bergson's analysis, which ends by imagining a time whose representation is made up of images of unequal tension, placed in a series according to degree of tension, and whose tension is regulated by action and its constraints. But can the superficial examination of a single order of facts assure us that only similar agglomerations of particular images and the variable tension to which these images are susceptible enter into the representation of time, at the point in its development at which we are trying to apprehend it? If this is so, we shall willingly leave the last word to the philosophers, asking them to explain the facts which have given us pause for thought. Are they able to do so?

When all is said and done, it is natural for philosophers to reduce the primordial elements of the notion of time to very simple terms. Is not their object to smash the heavy carapace of our mental operations, in order to release from it the reality it conceals? This hidden life of the human spirit is disclosed through the inconsistencies to which the logical play of superficial ideas leads. In the present case, the play of ideas, which disguises the psychological reality of successive images, consists in the adjustment of two series of representations. One is constant and periodic, that is, the calendar and chronology with their points of reference and all the details which they record: the other is perpetually being constructed through the contribution of new representations. The mind works constantly to associate certain elements of these two series within the same tension. The whole is dominated by general ideas of duration, period and date, which are endowed with a certain objectivity and which, with this objectivity, enter as essential elements into the mental operations in question.

This artificial schematisation is precisely one of the objects of study which interests us as sociologists for what it involves is the fixed, the resistant, the conceptual and the learnt. Moreover, in limiting ourselves to the domain of religion and magic, the problem that causes us concern is whether its formation and functioning can be explained without assuming anything more than recorded images and the variable tension of the individual consciousness which embraces them, or whether it is necessary to invoke some other principle, which is not completely represented in the consciousness of the individual but develops and operates in the course of collective life. In order to dispense with this last hypothesis, it would be necessary to show that the calendar only records the experiences of individuals and that in the light of practice the tension of the images accounts for the harmony constantly created between the two psychological series considered. Let us see, therefore, whether the constitution of the fixed series of images classed in time really presupposes individual experience alone.

5

It is generally believed that we experience the division of time through certain easily observable astronomical phenomena. In fact, there are two ways of determining the divisions of time, which are used concurrently. On the one hand, calendrical limits are made to coincide either with phenomena which indicate approximately the actual change of the seasons — the appearance of the first violet,[44] the first maybug, the first swallow,[45] of storks, of the song of the cuckoo,[46] etc. — or else with critical moments in the course of certain heavenly bodies, the moon, the sun, Sirius, Venus etc. In these various cases, it is incontestable that the signs chosen as an index of time are objects of experience. On the other hand, the points of division are marked by progressively counting a fixed number of units of time from one to another. Our system of weekly division is a perfect example of division running in numerically equal periods. In this case, the index of time appears to be entirely conventional at first sight. However, it is claimed that the generative numbers of calendrical periods are suggested by experimental knowledge of the actual length of certain astronomical periods.[47] What is more, the two processes are combined and, in a complete system of dividing time, one always finds numerical indexes associated with phenomenal indexes.

But the very use of these involves conventions. The choice of sign is already the object of an initial type of convention. The convention appears to be at a minimum when one is going by the course of the sun or moon, but it is preponderant when it is a matter of choosing between the multiple phenomena of vegetable or animal life which mark the fluctuating limits of the seasons. One preliminary convention fixes the choice on the swallow, cuckoo, stork or violet. Others aim at making the sign observed by a small number valid for all. There exist rules for the observation of the signs in question[48] and others for the purpose of consecrating, legitimising and authorising the observation made.

The use of astronomical indexes also leaves much room for the arbitrary. As regards the length of the lunar month, one initial source of uncertainty derives from the fact that it does not always begin at the same hour of the day, another from the fact that the sidereal and synodic revolutions of the moon differ by approximately two days.[49] This difference has really preoccupied and troubled peoples who have taken the lunar month as the basis of their calendar. Many have been driven to choose between the discrepancies of their experience, or to reconcile them by attributing an average length to the lunar month. The limits of the solar revolution are still more difficult to fix than those of the lunar revolution. They can only be determined with the aid of reference points and reliable instruments, following lengthy, patiently accumulated observations. The astronomical reputation of the Assyro–Babylonians led to their calendar being considered the perfect example of a system for the division of time based on the motion of the heavenly bodies. Now doubt has recently been expressed that their year of 365 days was originally a purely solar year based on experiment.[50] Parallel to this year of 365 days, they are known to have had a civic year of 360 days, whose basic element was apparently a period of 60 days, corresponding to the sexagesimal basis of their numeration and their metric system.[51] The annual cycle formed by the multiplication of this numerical base was brought into approximate agreement with the actual solar year. In the same way, Mexican cycles, founded on the numerical bases of 13 and 20, were brought into approximate agreement with the Venusian period, and elsewhere too, conventional agreements were established between the lunar month of 29 days and the schematic month of 30 days.[52] Experience, which gave birth to the divisions of time founded on astronomy, is aided by the existence of preliminary conventional calculations, which have allowed the length of astral revolutions to be determined: in a way, it is presented as the verification of a prediction.

To avoid appearing arbitrary, one could doubtless take refuge behind a theory of the experimental origin of ritual numbers. It could be said, for example, that the numbers 7 and 9 are obtained by the division, respectively into four and three parts, of the synodic revolution of the moon on the one hand and the sidereal revolution on the other.[53]

Some time ago, Americanists told us that it was possible to obtain these numbers in other ways, that is by adding up the cardinal points of space,[54] that these sums were represented by different symbols which served to represent total space in the ritual, and that the swastika was one of these symbols, corresponding to the number 9. Nothing prevents us from accepting that these same numbers were composed in the same way in western Asia and Europe, where, moreover, the mystical swastika is also found and, in precisely these places, the number 9 is employed as a ritual number. From now on, the study of the numeration of primitive peoples will lead us to cast doubt on the idea that numbers of this kind and, more generally, those which serve as bases for systems of numeration — in short, all those which are considered to be of particular importance — may be the fortuitous result of counting objects.[55] On the contrary, I regard them as subjective syntheses made by entire societies, each synthesis being capable of representing any whole, even the universe, without this whole breaking down naturally into as many parts as the number in question comprises smaller units. A similar theory assumes that numbers originally had exactly, so far as we know, the same value they had in late arithmetical mysticism. If this is so, there will be no difficulty in admitting that the numbers which govern the division of time are essentially conventional.

In brief, the division of time entails the maximum of convention and the minimum of experience. Ultimately, concrete experience lends it additional authority. But care for experimental accuracy, which is sometimes applied to the calendar, never lasts long. Just as, in astrology,[56] actual observations give way to charts of simplified observations mechanically applied, so too in the matter of time, the need to verify the coincidence of calendrical periods and astral periods progressively ceases to be felt necessary. The limits of the official year move imperceptibly away from the limits of the actual year. Thus the lunar week of the Chaldeans turned into the present week of the Hebrews.

We are unable to witness the primitive conventions that laid down the basic limits of calendars. But we can come close to them by establishing how social authority intervenes in their functioning. In Mesopotamia, the uncertainties over the actual beginning of the lunation were settled by the royal astrologers in charge of recording omens,[57] in Judea through sacerdotal authority with the agreement of the people,[58] and in Rome by the pontiffs.[59] What we know of the debates which arose in societies which hesitated between several markers of time[60] teaches us that objective experience did not necessarily impose them as the regulators of durations. Finally, every time we see the old calendars fallen into disuse themselves but long surviving in religion and magic, we receive a fair idea of the authority given to these indexes by the conventions which laid them down.

Other days are qualified than those which are the limits of the division of time. A good number seem to owe their qualities to certain events which are once supposed to have taken place on the same date. Thus in the Roman calendar, the anniversary of the defeat of Allia is an inauspicious day. In Christianity, in so far as the qualities of the days depend on the saints who preside over them, they appear equally to result from commemorated historical events, such as the death or deposition of the saint or the foundation of his sanctuary. Likewise, Friday, being the day of the Crucifixion, owes some of its qualities to the event being commemorated at that time. At least in the common view, therefore, the association between dates and their qualities in these different cases is based on general experiences, which apparently differ in no way from the experiences of individuals. But it is always possible to wonder whether a festival of historical commemoration is not an old festival rejuvenated, like that of St Martin on November 11th, or whether the qualification of the day being considered does not derive from quite different associations. For example, Friday [French *vendredi*, Ed.] has remained the day of the planet Venus. Here too, one falls back on convention. Thus the dates of observances whose institution has been explained by events in history are many, but there are very few that have no other reason to exist. As a general rule, it is not events that fix dates. Dates are times marked by a rhythm, which divides an indefinite duration into finite durations. In the same way, a rhythm determines the repetition *ad infinitum* of established dates, whatever they may be. The representation of time is essentially rhythmic.

But has it not already been demonstrated that, in work, poetry and song, rhythm was the sign of collective activity, becoming more strongly marked as social collaboration spread and intensified?[61] If this is true, it is legitimate to suppose that the rhythm of time does not necessarily model itself on the natural periodicities established by experience,

71

but that societies contain within themselves the need and the means of instituting it.

6

If the choice which determines qualified days is arbitrary, their particular qualification itself is no less so. Their qualities, being defined as they are by the sympathetic association of dates and their effects, whether positive or negative, are conventional in the same sense as all other sorts of sympathetic associations.[62] Among a multitude of possible associations, it is the arbitrary that decides, and this arbitrariness is not that of an individual who chooses for himself, but of whole societies.

Again, if we are concerned here with sympathetic associations between facts considered as necessarily concomitant, something other than the associated images must enter into these associations. We must expect to see the idea of magical power, of *mana* or the sacred, intervene in some way, establishing the belief of which other associations of the same type are the object in magic and religion. The associations which define the qualities of time must have a sacred character, like the terms of which they are composed: in other words, dates and their signs must have magico–religious power, and things signified, events or actions, participate in the nature of this power. This indefinite but very real entity — which is, as we have said elsewhere,[63] neither substance, nor quality nor action, but all these things together — must, like lightning, appear under one or other of the forms it is capable of assuming. This is briefly what I am going to confirm. Now this idea of the sacred, as we have already half–demonstrated, cannot form itself in the mind of the individual as such: it results from the subjective experiences of the collectivity.

To begin with, let us note that although the qualification of any date may appear to be defined by a limited number of sympathetic, imperative or persuasive associations, this limitation is only apparent. Certainly, for any given date in a given area, there is a fixed nucleus of prescriptions and expectations; but the list of them lengthens in proportion to the growing list of records.[64] In reality, dates attract actions and images to themselves by reason of the attention of which they are the object. They are invested with a sort of general qualification which is expressed in particular determinations. The latter, moreover, are often confused and sometimes totally effaced in the generality of the common qualification.

Without detracting from what I have said about the necessary association between events and times, we must recognise that qualified days are exchangeable and that rites move from one to another. Throughout the history of popular festivals in Europe, we have witnessed endless exchanges between St Martin, St Michael, St Nicholas, Christmas, Twelfth Night, St Anthony, etc. The different qualities of the qualified days are, on the whole, degrees and modes of the same quality. What is more, this quality is ambiguous and produces the contradictory effects which, for some years now, we have observed that sacred things are capable of. We have already arrived at a similar conclusion elsewhere in studying the properties of magic.[65] Thus we find a common quality behind the distinctive qualities of the parts of time, namely that of the sacred, to which these qualities are exactly reduced, as soon as we disregard the special associations which are attached to dates and periods, or as soon as they are multiplied *ad infinitum*. We must not think that to affirm this common trait is tantamount to denying their fundamental heterogeneity, for we know that this generic quality is susceptible to degrees and modes which are sufficient as a principle of differentiation. Besides, we know that by definition, sacred things also have a reason for being differentiated, since they only remain sacred by virtue of the constant effort needed to distinguish them first of all from the profane, and subsequently from one another.

If we now consider the imperative prescriptions of which dates are the object, we find other indications of the sacred character attached to them. Rites of entry and exit, which I have mentioned above, are one of them: in this respect the durations they frame are comparable to sacred ceremonies.

The peculiarity of sacred things is to be surrounded by prohibitions. Now, besides the special prohibitions attached to certain qualified dates, there are general prohibitions on activity which periodically bear on time. A typical example is the Sabbath,[66] as is the annual period when loss of power immobilised warriors in Ulster.[67] Concentrated at certain points of the calendar, these prohibitions — by virtue of the already known fact that the sacred is eminently moveable, and by reason of the close relationships which unite the dates in question with the durations that follow them — can be considered as ransoming these same durations from an interdict which would affect them equally.[68] From this, it follows that these durations appear to us in their turn as invested with one of the essential characteristics of the sacred. If we were to follow this reasoning, we would arrive at the notion of an essentially religious time, dangerous and solemn, which would remain unsuited to action if the interdict affecting it as a whole could not be lifted momentarily and completely distributed among some of its parts. This notion would be the almost concrete representation of a pure duration, existing in itself and entirely objective, at least as regards human actions, since the rhythm of its passing would not be marked by their succession. Furthermore, this duration, no less inert, immobile and slumbering than man, whose fearful torpor it imprisons, would be a veritable eternity. Here only the necessity to act in order to live, by carving from it successive eternities — shrunken images, yet perfect substitutes for the greatest eternity — would engender time.

When all is said and done, qualified days are festivals, and it is perhaps because there is no day which may not be qualified in some way that, in Latin, the word *feria* came to designate each of the days of the week. In any case, the critical dates of the calendar have the same qualitative nature as festivals proper. It is evident either that they are chosen for the celebration of rites or that rites sanctify them. Their religious character manifests itself in the same way as that of festivals through positive rites, prohibitions,[69] the presence of the supernatural,[70] in a word, through everything that constitutes the abnormal,[71] through everything that can distinguish them from the mass of days which pass unnoticed. Conversely, festivals proper have been or tend to be the pivots of the calendar. This balancing, this exchange of characteristics and functions between calendrical dates and festivals, is particularly easy to observe during periods of uncertainty, such as the first centuries of the Middle Ages, in which an equilibrium between Roman, Christian, Germanic and Celtic institutions was being established in northern and western Europe. We see, for example, January 1st, the festival of the Calends positively assume the characteristics of a festival like that of St John[72] — and, on the other hand, festivals without any calendrical function originally, such as Easter and Christmas, are progressively substituted, as limits of the division of time, for old seasonal festivals such as that of St Martin.

Thus the parts of time in which religious things take place are as sacred as these things themselves. This essential convention governs the formation of the conventions listed to begin with, whose precise object is to define the conditions for realising this quality of the sacred, which is linked to time, with the various modifications of which it is capable. In short, the qualitative picture of time is formed by a large number of conventions which by abstraction, establish relations of cause and effect between actually occurring phenomena and time itself, relations which are, in the last analysis, relations of identity.

7

But in finding the idea of the sacred at the root of the qualitative representations recorded in this picture, we arrive at a strong presumption that the emotional and logical conditions under which the idea of time in magic and religion might be developed are very different from those under which, it seems, this idea must normally appear in individuals. On the assumption that this idea arose ready formed in each man separately, these conditions are such that it must have been subjected to remarkable modifications. In fact, it is necessary to take account of those states of collective excitement in which, formerly, we supposed the idea of the sacred to be formed. The profound modifications, which our own emotions bring to our consciousness, of the duration help us to imagine how the multiple emotions of a society could have affected the consciousness of all its members in the same way, but with greater intensity and for a longer period. These primitive emotions, exceptional and momentary, have left behind them a residue of belief which renews or maintains certain of their effects when their cause has largely disappeared. They are perpetuated and continue to condition thought through the logical force of categories and concepts.

In these different ways, the notion of the sacred enters as a disturbing element into judgements concerning time. By the very fact that it introduces into their terms the idea of a magical power which is only limited by itself, it justifies all possible anomalies *a priori*. On the other hand, its known properties allow us to explain analytically those which were identified at the start of this work as the properties of the magico–religious idea of time. We have already seen that they cease to be contradictory if we substitute the idea of qualitative time for that of quantitative time, especially since it is the former which is fundamentally capable of being sacred. As far as the qualitative homogeneity of the parts of time is concerned, it is not only absurd to imagine that these parts, being distinct, cannot, each in itself, be qualitatively homogeneous, it is also criminal, a sacrilege, to upset this sacred homogeneity, the same crime as breaking a taboo. The symmetrical parts are not merely equivalent to the extent that they are qualitatively similar, but, by reason of the ease with which the sacred is substantialised in being objectified, they are really and substantially identical. It is natural for a part of a duration to be taken for the whole, not only because the quality with which the whole is invested is also found entire in the parts, but basically because the quality of this duration can be detached from it and fixed to its part. Finally, critical dates interrupt durations because, on the one hand, being sacred, they really are what they are literally, that is to say, separative, and, on the other — for the same reason — they entail the inhibitions that all sacred things bring with them, and of which the prohibitions of the Sabbath are typical.

The reply to the question posed at the beginning of this study is that magic and religion have reconciled the flagrant contradiction between the notion of the sacred and the notion of time, to the demands of which they are equally subject, by conventionally attributing the quality of being sacred to time and its parts, moments and periods. They have put the sacred into time and in this way have established the uninterrupted chain of eternities along which their rites can be dispersed and reproduced while remaining unalterably identical.

8

The expressions I have just used can only be convincing if it is assumed that, apart from the collective labour that gives magical and religious time its qualitative value, individuals are provided with a notion of time which each of them separately has abstracted from his or her consciousness. But among the subjective experiences that have instructed them, it is necessary to include those generated in the midst of an exalted collectivity. We already know how objectively subjective representation, the consciousness of magical power, frees itself through abstraction from these states of exaltation in semi—concrete or entirely concrete and personal forms. Everything which, under the same conditions, is the object of the same intense attention lends itself to the same phenomena of abstraction and generalisation: one sees them being produced in the series of sympathetic associations, but with differing degrees of elaboration.[73] As for time, just as the general notion of *mana* which is the order of efficacies, has emerged from the consciousness of particular efficacies, so perhaps the general notion of time, the order of possible concomitances, has freed itself from the acute perception of changing concomitances. The facts relating to consciousness in question are objectivised because they coincide in the consciousness of many, who are simultaneously conscious of their agreement and of its inevitability. The objectivity of these facts follows from their shared and experienced subjectivity. On the other hand, their abstraction is parallel to their objectivisation. Finally, the first idea, that of *mana* or the sacred, lends some of its reality to the second, that of time. But given that the conditions of the mystical environment are such that any conception within it turns into efficacy and reality, whenever there is occasion to conceive of the abstract and general idea of time in this environment, this time finds itself realized absolutely. From this it again follows that religious events which take place in time are legitimately and logically considered to be taking place in eternity.

I do not know whether the same abstraction could have been created in other circumstances, though I do not deny it. I claim only to show that the latter are particularly favourable to its production, by reason, first, of the objectivity they are capable of giving it, and also, because they lend themselves to the formation of the conventions that create words, without which there is no valid abstraction. The abstraction emerging from this would correspond with the characteristics of the notion of time, since its creation would parallel that of a system of successive points, defined by the concomitances described, and whose relative positions, regulated by the law of rhythm — since this is a matter of social representations — would constitute a picture of time.

On the assumption that the conditions stated above — the power of abstracting and generalising, the establishment of common coincidences, the collective work of consciousness, notions of the sacred and of magical power — are sufficient to give magic and religion the idea of time they demonstrate, should we infer that the same phenomena of collective action are necessary to the formation of the notion of time which functions in our consciousness, outside any preoccupation with magic or religion? I am very far from claiming this, and I have no interest in speculating on it. In any case, if we consider not what is simplest and most abstract in our notion of time, but the actual complexity of those of our representations in which the notion is implied in such a way that it arises from the past and from tradition, it is incontestable that the special forms of this notion which have just been examined have largely contributed to the elaboration of the others.

Besides, our actual representation of time — which, as I said, implies a sort of fixed catalogue, whose points appear to have the property of rising one after the other into the present of our consciousness — is imperfectly separated or, at least, only separated by an abstraction, itself imperfect, from our system of measuring time and especially from the calendar. Now the true original function of calendars is actually religious or magico–religious. Calendars served essentially to predict the return of events which were believed necessarily to entail the celebration of certain rites or the production of the sort of phenomenon to which religion address itself. Although it may be difficult to prove that they really were instituted to ensure the regular observation of the inevitable concomitances of images and of rites, one can nonetheless see that the object of the modifications to which they have given rise, even quite recently, has been the rediscovery of the regularity of these concomitances. This constitutes strong presumptive evidence, at least, concerning the nature of their first institution. The aim of the Julian and Gregorian reforms of the calendar was essentially religious. It was equally for religious reasons that these reforms were not accepted without opposition and that something always survives of calendars that have been abolished. The authority of the convention which creates the calendar gives it a reality equal to that of the phenomena which, it is claimed, regulate it. In brief, the calendar is the order of the periodicity of rites. On the other hand, its history teaches us that it encodes the qualities of time. The first calendars were almanacs, which recorded, day by day, magico–religious predictions and prescriptions.[74]

Thus the institution of the calendar has not as its sole, nor doubtless its main object the measurement of the flow of time, considered as a quantity. It originates not in the idea of a purely quantitative time, but in that of qualitative time, composed of discontinuous parts, heterogeneous and ceaselessly revolving, whose characteristics I set out above. Truth to tell — and taking everything into account — the sustained fruitfulness of this second notion was calculated to produce the first. The multiplication of qualified points, the progressive differentiation of countable parts, the very confusion of qualities, which I have already described, had to lead to the analysis of the initial syntheses. In short, the work of abstraction, from which the notion of objective, quantitative and abstract time arose, is perhaps a consequence of the work which has separated qualitative and semi–concrete time from things.

Essay on time

NOTES

1. *L'Année sociologique* [hereafter *A.S.*] V, 1902, Introduction to review section, "Le Rituel": 247–8, at 248.

2. Henri Hubert and Marcel Mauss, "Esquisse d'une théorie générale de la magie", *A.S.* VII, 1904: 1–146, at 108 ff.

3. Henri Hubert and Marcel Mauss, "Essai sur la nature et la fonction sociale du sacrifice", A.S. II, 1899: 29–138; id., "Magie", 1ff.; Marcel Mauss, "L'Origine des pouvoirs magiques dans les sociétés australiennes", *Annuaire de l'Ecole Pratique des Hautes Etudes*, 1904: 1–55, passim.

4. Hubert and Mauss, "Sacrifice": 56; "Magie": 47.

5. Johann Friedrich Hermann Gunkel, *Zum religions-geschichtlichen Verständniß des neuen Testaments*, Göttingen 1903: 22.

6. William Warde Fowler, *The Roman Festivals of the Period of the Republic,* London 1899: 176.

7. Giuseppe Pitrè, *Feste patronali in Sicilia*, Torino and Palermo 1900 49, passim; cf. Henri Hubert, Review of Pitrè, *A.S.* IV: 245–8, at 246; Richard Wünsch, *Das Frühlingsfest der Insel Malta: ein Beitrag zur Geschichte der Antiken Religion*, Leipzig 1902: 29 (in which the festival of St Gregory replaced the festival of St John).

8. Sir Edmund Kerchever Chambers, *The Mediaeval Stage*, Oxford 1903 (2 vols.): Ch. IX ("The Sword–Dance"); Pitrè, passim.

9. Sir John Rhys, *Celtic Folklore: Welsh and Manx*, Oxford 1901 (2 vols.): Ch. VIII ("Welsh Cave Legends"), 473 ff.

* These notes follow the style of Hubert's presentation, with editorial additions.

83

Henri Hubert

10. Elard Hugo Meyer, *Mythologie der Germanen gemeinfaßlich dargestellt*, Strassburg 1903: 386.

11. Gustav Bilfinger, *Untersuchungen über die Zeitrechnung der alten Germanen*, Stuttgart 1886, I, "Das altnordische Jahr": 1 ff.

12. On periodic limitation of stay among the spirits, see Johann Wilhelm Emmanuel Mannhardt, *Germanische Mythen Forschungen*, Berlin 1858: 172, 177; Paul Yves Sébillot, *Le folklore de France*, Paris 1904–7 (4 vols): Vol. 1, 305, 463 etc.

13. George Frederick Abbott, *Macedonian Folklore*, Cambridge 1903: 277.

14. Wilhelm Heinrich Roscher, *Die enneadischen und hebdomadischen Fristen und Wochen der ältesten Griechen*, Abh. d. ph. h. hl. d. kgt. sächs. Gesellschaft der Wissenschaften, Vol. XXI, Leipzig 1903; Johann Heinrich Graf, *Über Zahlenaberglauben insbesondere die Zahl 13*, Bern 1904: 16 ff.

15. Plutarch, *Lives, Agis* II.

16. Roscher, ibid.: 22; cf. Karl Otfried Müller, *Die Dorier*, Breslau 1824: 100. For other examples of the same periodicity being imposed on magistracies, see Arthur Bernard Cook, "The European Sky–God II", *Folk–lore* XV, 4, 1904: 369–426, at 394 ff.

17. Roscher, ibid.: passim.

18. Warde Fowler, ibid.: 33 ff. (*mensis Martius*), 277 ff. (*mensis Januarius*). On the auspicious character of rites at the start of the year, see Macrobius, *Saturnalia* I: xii, 6; Ovid, *Fasti* III: 135.

19. James George Frazer, *The Golden Bough*, 2nd ed., London 1900 (3 vols.): Vol. II, 70 ff.; Vol. III, 95 ff.

20. For example, the septenary rhythm of education in Greece: see pseudo–Plato, *Axiochus*: 3660; Plato, *Alcibiades* I: 121e; Quintilian, *Institutio Oratoria* I: i, 15.

21. Caesar, *De Bello Gallico* I: 50.

22. Herodotus VI: 106.

23. Zenobius III: 79: ἐντὸς ἑβδόμης ["before the seventh of the month"]; cf. Hesychius, *Suidas*; Xenophon, *Anabasis* I: vii, 18: the soothsayer Silanus assures the young Cyrus ὅτι βασιλεύς οὐ μαχεῖται δέκα ἡμερῶν ["that the king will not fight within ten days"; transl. C.L. Brownson, Cambridge Mass. and London 1921].

24. Theophrastus, 6 *De Signis Tempestatum*, ß: 8: ἐὰν ἕωθεν ἀστράπτη εἴωθε παύεσθαι τριταῖος [ὁ νότος], οἱ δὲ ἄλλοι πεμπταῖοι, ἑβδομαῖοι, ἐνναταῖοι (following the local rhythms of the division of time) ["A wind rising in the early morning, if accompanied by lightning, generally ceases on the third day; other [such] winds cease on the fifth, seventh or ninth day"; transl. J.G. Wood, London 1894; Wood says that he based this passage on Gottlob Schneider's text (Leipzig 1818), in preference to Frederick Wimmer's text (Paris 1866); Hubert appears to have used the latter here — Ed.]; id.: 6, a, 8: μεταβάλλει γὰρ ὡς ἐπὶ τὸ πολύ ἐν τῇ τετράδι, ἐὰν δὲ μὴ ἐν τῇ ὀγδόῃ, εἰ δὲ μὴ πανσέληνῳ... ["The change takes place for the most part on the fourth day; and if not then, on the first quarter; and if not then, at the full," etc.; transl. op. cit.].

25. Karl Friedrich Adolf Wuttke, *Der deutsche Volksaberglaube der Gegenwart*, 2nd revised ed., Berlin 1869: 75.

26. Wuttke, ibid.; Mannhardt, ibid.: 519 ("The hour of the vow" returning every seven days, Islinsk aefintyri, 44).

27. Wuttke, ibid.; Jakob Ludwig Karl Grimm, *Deutsche Mythologie*,

Henri Hubert

4th ed., Berlin 1875–8 (3 vols.): III, 441, no. 197; cf. ibid.: II, 563 ff.

28. Wuttke, ibid.; Edwin Sidney Hartland, *The Legend of Perseus: A Study of Tradition in Story, Custom and Belief*, London 1894–6 (3 vols.): II, 119, 125 etc.; Pliny, *Natural History*, XXVIII: 260; cf. Martial, *Epigrams* V: xxix, 1; *Hist. Aug., Alexander Severus*: 38.

29 Wuttke, ibid.; Grimm, ibid.: III, 446, no. 374; cf. C. Heuillard, "Traditions et superstitions de la Champagne", *Revue des Traditions Populaires*, XIX, 1904: 22 (under "Le Coucou"); Léon Pineau, "Le Folk-lore de la Touraine, VI", *Revue des Traditions Populaires*, XIX, 1904: 293–5, at 294; Alfred de Nore [= Adolphe de Chesnel], *Coutumes, mythes et traditions des provinces de France*, Paris 1846: 263.

30. *Mal*, evil: Hermann Paul, *Deutsches Wörterbuch*, Halle 1896–7: 292; Friedrich Kluge, *Etymologisches Wörterbuch der deutschen Sprache*, Strassburg 1883 (5th ed. 1894): 257: *Dheihs, thing = tempus*; cf. Friedrich Kluge and F. Lutz, *English Etymology: A Select Glossary*, Strassburg 1898: 210. *Stunde:* Grimm, *Deutsche Mythologie*: II, 660.

31. Karl Adam Heinrich Kellner, *Heortologie; oder, Die geschichtliche Entwicklung des Kirchenjahres und der Heiligenfeste*, 2nd edn., Freiburg 1906: 26 ff. [English translation, *Heortology: A History of the Christian Festivals*, London 1908].

32. Ibid.: 2 ff.

33. Albrecht Friedrich Weber, *Zwei vedische Texte über Omina und Portenta*, Berlin 1859: 388; id., ed., "Drittes Buch der Atharva–Samhita", *Indische Studien* (Berlin) XVII, 2–3, 1885: 177–314, at 224; Vedische Beiträge, *Sitzungsberichte d. kgl. pr. Ak. d. Wiss. zu Berlin, ph. h. Kl.*, XXXVII, 1898: 558–81, at 559–60. I do not accept the equivalence proposed

by Weber between the first twelve days of every month and the *Dodekahemeron* of the Christian year.

34. Roscher, *Fristen und Wochen*: passim.

35. Mannhardt, *Germanische Mythen*: 446 (seven days = seven years); Sébillot, *Le folk-lore de France*: I, 257, 465.

36. Cf. Georg Friedrich Thibaut, "Astronomie, Astrologie und Mathematik", *Grundriß der Indo-Arischen Philologie*: Vol. III, part 9, 28.

37. Cf. Macrobius, *Saturnalia* I: xv: Aptitudes of the Calends, Ides and Nones; Plutarch, *Quaestiones Romanae*: 100: Festival of Diana Aventine (women washing their heads); de Nore, ibid.: 278: days to select and avoid for blood-letting.

38. Warde Fowler, ibid.: general observations on each month.

39. Henri Bergson, *Essais sur les données immédiates de la conscience*, Paris 1904 (4th ed.). [Note added by editor.]

40. Henri Bergson, *Matière et mémoire*, Paris 1896. [Note added by editor.]

41. On numerical symbolism, cf. Joannis Laurenti Lydii (Lydus), *Liber de mensibus* (ed. R. Wuensch, Lips 1898): I, 15; II, 6.

42. *Talmud Babli*: Sanhedr, 41b, 42a (hesitation relative to the actual length of the period during which the blessing of the new moon must be pronounced); cited by Friedrich Bohn, *Der Sabbat im Alten Testament und im altjüdischen religiösen Aberglauben*, Gutersloh 1903: 35. The two days of *Rosch haschana*, having given rise to the same hesitations, are considered to be "of one single sanctity"; Johannes Buxtorfius the Elder, *Synagoga Judaica*, Hanover 1604: 494.

43. Lydus, *Liber de mensibus*: III, 5, 9, 10. Cf. the attempt made to fix the date of Easter on a day determined by the Julian calendar, March 25th or 27th, Kellner, *Heortologie*: 39. Cf. F. Duine, "Coutumes et superstitions de la Haute–Bretagne", *Revue des traditions populaires* XIX, 1904: 112–14, at 113, and 243–8, at 244, 248; N. Guyot, "Le Folk–lore de la Côte d'Or", ibid.: 217–20, at 218; A. Harou, "Notes sur les traditions et légendes de la province de Liège": 296–303, at 301; Pineau, "Le Folk–lore de la Touraine, VII": 430–3, at 432.

44. Grimm, *Deutsche Mythologie*: Vol. II, 635 ff.

45. Cf. Atheneus, 4 Deipnosophists 5: VIII, 360 b,c.

46. Grimm: 605 ff., 636.

47. Roscher: 1 ff.

48. Grimm: 636; Hans Sachs, *Werke*, Tübingen 1870–1908 (26 vols.): IV, 3, 43 ff.; Niels Nikolaus Falck, *Neues Staatsbürgerliches Magazin* I (Schleswig, 1832): 655 (cited by Grimm, ibid.); Abbott, *Macedonian Folklore*: 16 ff.

49. Roscher: 4 ff.; *Talmud Babli*: Pesachim, 111a; ibid., Schabou'ot, 9a.

50. G. Kewitsch, "Zweifel an der astronomischen und geometrischen Grundlage des 60–Systems", *Zeitschift für Assyriologie und vorderasiatische Archäologie*, XIX, 1904: 73–95.

51. Cf. H. Winckler, "Die Weltanschauung des alten Orients", *Ex Oriente Lux* I, 1, 1904: 1–50, at 20; cf. Eduard Meyer, *Ægyptische Chronologie*, I, Berlin 1904: 1907.

52. Lydus, *Liber de mensibus* III: 14 (considerations of arithmetical mysticism concerning the number 30).

53. Roscher: ibid.

54. E.g. north, south, east, west, zenith, nadir, centre = 7. [Editor's note: this footnote was added to the reissued version and may reflect Mauss's influence; cf. E. Durkheim and M. Mauss, *Primitive Classification*, London: Cohen & West 1963 (1903), Ch. 3.]

55. W. J. McGee, "Primitive Numbers", *19th Annual Report of the Bureau of Ethnology* Part 2 [for 1897–8, but publ. 1900]: 821–51.

56. Auguste Bouché–Leclercq, *L'Astrologie grecque*, Paris 1899: 517 ff.

57. Reginald Campbell Thompson, *The Reports of the Magicians and Astronomers of Nineveh and Babylon in the British Museum*, London 1900 (2 vols): Introduction, xviii ff.

58. Emil Schürer, *Geschichte des jüdischen Volkes im Zeitalter Jesu Christi*, Leipzig 1890 (2 parts, 2nd ed.): I, 616 ff.

59. Varro, *De Lingua Latina* 6, 27; Macrobius, *Saturnalia* I: xv, 9.

60. On agreement between the lunar and solar systems, see Ben Siria: xliii, 1–10; Livre des Jubilés: c, vi, end; Talmud Babli, Sonkka: 29a, 6.

61. Karl Bücher, *Arbeit und Rhythmus*, Leipzig 1898 (2nd ed.); Francis Barton Gummere, *The Beginnings of Poetry*, New York 1901; cf. Marcel Mauss, Review of Gummere, *A.S.* VI: 560–5 at 560.

62. Hubert and Mauss, "Magie": 65ff.

63. Ibid.: 109.

64. Cf. Pineau, "Le Folk–lore de la Touraine, VII".

65. Hubert and Mauss, ibid.

66. The Sabbath is properly, as the etymology of the word indicates, the end of a period; cf. Bohn, *Sabbat*: 2.

67. Eleanor Hull, "Old Irish Tabus, or *Geasa*" *Folk–lore* XII, 1, 1901: 41–66, at 58. Cf. Giovanni Pinza, *La Conservazione delle teste umane e le idee ed i costumi coi quali si connette*, Rome 1898: 78; cf. Karl Sapper, "Religiöse Gebräuche der Kekchi–Indianer", *Archiv für Religionswissenschaft* VII, 3-4, 1904: 453–70, at 459.

68. Cf. H. Hubert and M. Mauss, Review of Morris Jastrow, *The Original Character of the Hebrew Sabbat, A.S.* II: 264–6, at 266; Marie Joseph Lagrange, *Etudes sur les religions sémitiques*, Paris 1905, 2nd ed.: 284.

69. Wuttke, *Deutsche Volksaberglaube*: 75; Sir Henry Creswicke Rawlinson, *The Cuneiform Inscriptions of Western Asia*, London 1861–84 (5 vols.; 2nd ed., London 1891): V, 48, 49.

70. On the special powers of certain beings on the critical dates, see Wuttke, ibid.; Eckhart, *Südhannoversches Sagenbuch*, Leipzig 1899: 28 (the power of children born on a Sunday). On the circulation of spirits, see Wuttke, ibid.; S. E. Peal, "Ein Ausflug nach Banpara", *Zeitschrift für Ethnologie* XXX, 1899: 281–371, at 355 (return of souls among the Naga, at the new moon in December); *Talmud Babli*, Baba Batra: 74a (return of souls every thirty days).

71. On the interruption of the social order at the ends of periods, cf. Gessert, *Globus* 1898: II, 250.

72. Franz Alexander Tille, *Yule and Christmas: Their Place in the Germanic Year*, London 1899: 81 ff. and passim.

73. Hubert and Mauss, "Magie": 61 ff.

74. Cf. François Joseph Chabas, *Le Calendrier des jours fastes et néfastes de l'année égyptienne: traduction complète du Papyrus Sallier IV*, Paris 1869.

REVIEW OF HUBERT'S ESSAY ON TIME*

Marcel Mauss

Hubert raises a question which is relevant to two very important problems: one is connected with the sociology of religion properly speaking, and the other with the general theory of collective representations. This short essay, which is the product of more extensive research than might appear at first sight, examines not only a certain number of the characteristics of the representation of time, but also shows how this representation is affected by the presence of the representation of the sacred.

Even the least well-informed among us can be in no doubt that time has not been represented in the same way in every religion and in all folklore. The scientific notion of a uniform succession of moments and durations — a notion which philosophers continue to speculate about — evolved only very slowly. On the one hand, it was constructed by the individual in accordance with the theory of errors well-known to psychologists, and also by the various series of societies which have succeeded each other during the course of history. On the other, it was discovered through the unidirectional progression of the sciences. It is only necessary to open a good book on the subject of China or India, to learn that in Hindu or Chinese philosophy, time is not conceived to be uniform, or homogeneous or a pure

*   Translated by Jacqueline Redding from a review of Hubert's "Etude sommaire de la représentation du temps dans la religion et la magie", *L'Année sociologique*, X, 1907: 302-304.

dimension. It is deemed to be made up of quantitatively and qualitatively dissimilar periods which cannot be superposed and which sometimes even succeed each other in no particular order.

This fact had never been adequately debated before the appearance of the work considered here. Hubert, however, does not restrict himself to doing this. He looks for the general forms of this primitive representation of time — which preceded the scientific notion — and he tries to find the very causes of the representation. To that end, he analyses facts borrowed from the Greek and Roman civilizations and from western folklore. In beginning a course on festivals with these considerations, he actually indicates the nature of the religious calendar. Even today, religious chronology remains caught in this limbo, for a significant part of our mental activity continues to depend on old ways of counting and classifying.

A certain number of propositions sum up the main observations. First, "critical dates interrupt the continuity of time", discontinuity being the determining factor of festivals. Second, "intervals bounded by two associated critical dates are, in themselves, continuous and indivisible". Whilst festivals interrupt time, the periods which end or begin with those very festivals are, by contrast, held to be endowed with such perfect continuity and perfect unity, that they even have personality ascribed to them. Third, not only is time not continuous, nor divisible, nor clearly defined, but religion and magic acknowledge that the critical date, that is to say basically a moment, represents an entire period. A festival is in fact symbolic of the whole of the duration which it governs, inaugurates or terminates: "critical dates are equivalent to the intervals they limit". Fourth, it is considered to be of the essence of time that its parts are not — unlike the parts of space — superposable, equivalent. Magic and religion have always thought otherwise: "similar parts are equivalent". One festival is worth another, is indeed identical with the other. A given week can be equivalent to the year; seemingly irreducible individualities are, on the contrary, subject to confusions and constant equivalences. Fifth, as a corollary to the previous proposition, "some quantitatively unequal durations are equalised and vice versa".

Not having given this question adequate consideration, we do not know whether these five, or more accurately four, theories cover all the facts. We believe so. But we suspect that the problem of the relationship between the idea of eternity and that of time cannot easily be resolved starting from these facts alone, and yet it is this problem which, in Hubert's own opinion, is of prime importance. We even suspect that his analysis, however complicated it might be, does not actually deal with the conflict which appears to exist between sacred moments and secular duration, between common time, festivals and those dates which seem to arise from substantial and eternal sanctity to divide everyday life into different periods of time. Does Hubert connect this problem with the narrower problem of festivals? We do not know whether he is right or wrong in not doing so here. In any case, it is a mistake not to indicate the reasons for the omission.

The second part of the work enquires into the causes of this notion of time. In such an essay, intended to suggest hypotheses rather than to establish the truth of them, this investigation was necessarily restricted. In any case, it is obvious that it could only come to a conclusion by actually analysing the festivals and the religious calendar, and that it would have been unwise to discuss the latter in terms of conclusions which the work itself had to provide. Hubert was, therefore, only able to outline two general ideas. One of these is a negative one, namely that the religious notion of time — which precedes the scientific notion of time — certainly does not originate in individuals and does not fall within the realm of psychology. The way it varies from society to society, the way it cannot be fitted into every index proposed for it, its arbitrary nature and conventional character, all demonstrate that it is social in origin and must be placed in the domain of sociology. But to what order of social causes shall we attach these primitive manifestations of the representation of time? The answer to our question is that this qualifying table of specific, equalised, connected and separate times, exists primarily to regulate religious practice. This practical characteristic itself originates in a fundamental law which not only guarantees religious life but the whole of social life: it is the law of collective rhythm, of rhythmic activity for social ends. Naturally Hubert was unable to develop fully this all too fruitful idea here.

BIBLIOGRAPHIES

1   WORKS BY HENRI HUBERT*

1897   "Observations sur la chronologie de Théophane et de quelques lettres des papes." *Byzantinische Zeitschrift*, VI: 491–505.

1899a   "Etude sur la formation des Etats de l'Eglise. Les papes Grégoire II, Grégoire III, Zacharie, Etienne III et leurs relations avec les empereurs iconoclastiques." *Revue historique*, LXIX: 1–40, 241–272.

1899b   "Fibules de Basilieux." *Revue archéologique*, 1: 363–381.

1899c   (with M. Mauss) "Essai sur la nature et la fonction du sacrifice." *L'Année sociologique*, II: 29–138. Reprinted in Hubert and Mauss 1909a.

1899d   (with M. Mauss) Review of M. Jastrow, *The Original Character of the Hebrew Sabbat. L'Année sociologique* II: 264–6.

1900   "Kyrèné." *Dictionnaire des antiquités grecques et romaines*, III: 873–880.

1901a   Review of W. W. Fowler, *The Roman Festivals of the Period of the Republic. L'Année sociologique*, IV: 234–9.

1901b   Review of Pitrè, *Feste patronali in Sicilia. L'Année sociologique*, IV: 245–8.

1902a   Introduction to the section on ritual, *L'Année sociologique*, V: 247–8.

---

*   For a more comprehensive bibliography, see Lantier 1928.

1902b "La Collection Moreau au Musée de Saint-Germain." *Revue archéologique*, 2: 167–208.

1904a "Magia." *Dictionnaire des antiquités grecques et romaines*, VI: 1134–1138.

1904b Introduction to *Manuel d'histoire des religions* de Chantepie de la Saussaye, Paris, Colin: v–xlvii.

1904c (with M. Mauss) "Esquisse d'une théorie générale de la magie." *L'Année sociologique*, VII: 1–46.

1905 "Etude sommaire de la représentation du temps dans la religion et la magie." *Annuaire de l'Ecole Pratique des Hautes Etudes, Section des Sciences Religieuses*: 1–39. Reprinted in Hubert and Mauss 1909a.

1906a (with M. Mauss) "Introduction à l'analyse de quelques phénomènes religieux." *Revue de l'histoire des religions*, LVIII: 163–203. Reprinted in Hubert and Mauss 1909a.

1906b "La Collection Moreau au Musée de Saint-Germain." *Revue archéologique*, 2: 337–371.

n.d. "Mithra." *Grande Encyclopédie*, XXIII: 1134–1138.

1909a (with M. Mauss) *Mélanges d'histoire des religions*, Paris: Alcan.

1909b Review of S. Reinach, *Orpheus. L'Anthropologie*, XX: 596.

1910a "La Commission des monuments préhistoriques." *L'Anthropologie*, XXI: 21–331.

1910b "L'Origine des aryens. A propos des fouilles américaines du Turkestan." *L'Anthropologie*, XXI: 519–528.

1912a   "Nantosuelta, déesse de la ruche." *Mélanges Cagnat*, Paris: Leroux. Reprinted in 1925b.

1912b   "Le Carnassier androphage et la représentation de l'Océan chez les Celtes." *Compte rendu de la XIVe session du congrès international d'anthropologie et d'archéologie préhistoriques* (Genève): 220–230.

1913   "Notes d'archéologie et de philologie celtique." *Revue celtique*, XXXIV: 1–13, 424–425.

1914a   "Notes d'archéologie et de philologie celtique." *Revue celtique*, XXXV: 14–43.

1914b   "Les Projets de loi sur les fouilles." *L'Anthropologie* XXV: 345–365.

1914c   "Le Culte des héros et ses conditions sociales." *Revue de l'histoire des religions*, LXX: 1–20.

1915a   "Le Culte des héros et ses conditions sociales." *Revue de l'histoire des religions*, LXXI: 195–247.

1915b   "Une nouvelle Figure du dieu au maillet." *Revue achéologique*, I: 26–39.

1919   Preface to S. Czarnowski, *Le Culte des héros et ses conditions sociales. Saint Patrick, héros national de l'Irelande*, Paris: Alcan: i–xciv.

1925a   "Le Mythe d'Epona." *Mélanges linguistiques offerts à J. Vendryès*, Paris: Champion: 187–211.

1925b   *Divinités gauloises, Sucellus et Nantosuelta, Epona, dieux de l'autre monde.* Mâcon: Prolat.

1927   "Les prières Celtes en Espagne." *Revue celtique*, XLIV: 78–89.

1932a   *Les Celtes et l'expansion celtique jusqu'à l'époque de la Tène*. Paris: Corbeil (Collection, l'Evolution de l'humanité, XXVI). New edition 1950 (reprinted 1974) Paris: Albin Michel.

1932b   *Les Celtes depuis l'époque de la Tène et la civilisation celtique*. Paris: Corbeil (Collection, l'Evolution de l'humanité, XXVII). New edition 1950 (reprinted 1974) Paris: Albin Michel.

1934a   *The Rise of the Celts*. London: Kegan Paul & Co.

1934b   *The Greatness and Decline of the Celts*. London: Kegan Paul & Co.

1952   *Les Germains*. Paris: Albin Michel.

1979   Texte autobiographique de Henri Hubert. *Revue française de sociologie*, XX, 1: 205–207.

2   WORKS ON HENRI HUBERT

Berr, H. 1906 "Les Progrès de la sociologie religieuse." *Revue de synthèse historique,* XII: 16–43.

Berr, H. 1932a Foreword to Hubert 1932a.

Berr, H. 1932b Foreword to Hubert 1932b.

Chalus, P. 1952 Foreword to Hubert 1952.

Drouin, M. 1929 "Henri Hubert." *Association de secours des anciens élèves de l'Ecole Normale Supérieure*: 45–51.

Isambert, F.-A. 1979 "Henri Hubert et la sociologie du temps." *Revue française de sociologie,* XX, 1: 183–204.

Lantier, R. 1928 "Hommage à Henri Hubert et bibliographie d'Henri Hubert." *Revue archéologique,* XVIII, 2: 289–307.

Mauss, M. 1907 Review of Hubert 1905.

Mauss, M. 1950 Preface to Hubert 1932.

Reinach, S. 1927 "Henri Hubert." *Revue archéologique,* XVII: 176–178.

Saintyves, P. 1919 "Les notions de temps et d'éternité dans la magie et la religion." *Revue de l'histoire des religions,* 179: 75–104.

Strenski, I. 1987 "Henri Hubert, Racial Science and Political Myth." *Journal of the History of Behavorial Sciences,* 23: 353–367.

Strenski, I. 1991 "Hubert, Mauss and the Comparative Social History of Religions." In M. Despland, ed., *La Tradition française en sciences religieuses.*

Varagnac, A. 1963 "Au musée des antiquités nationales, la rétrospective Broglie, Hubert et Mauss." *Antiquités nationales et internationales,* janv.–mars: 1–24.

Vendryès, J. 1927 "Henri Hubert." *Revue Celtique*: 500–502.

3   GENERAL BIBLIOGRAPHY

Abbott, G. F. 1903 *Macedonian Folklore*. Cambridge: Cambridge University Press.

Bergson, H. 1896 *Matière et mémoire*. Paris: Alcan.

Bergson, H. 1904 *Essai sur les données immédiates de la conscience*, 4th edn. Paris: Alcan.

Berr, H. 1906 "Les Progrès de la sociologie religieuse." *Revue de synthèse historique*, XII: 16–43.

Berr, H. 1932a. Foreword to Hubert 1932a.

Berr, H. 1932b. Foreword to Hubert 1932b.

Bilfinger, G. 1886 *Untersuchungen über die Zeitrechnung der alten Germanen.* Stuttgart: Liebich.

Bohn, F. 1903 *Der Sabbat im Alten Testament und im altjüdischen religiösen Aberglauben*. Gutersloh: Bertelsmann.

Bouché–Leclercq, A. 1899 *L'astrologie grecque*. Paris: Leroux.

Bücher, K. 1898 *Arbeit und Rhythmus*, 2nd edn. Leipzig: Teubner.

Chabas, F. J. 1869 *Le calendrier des jours fastes et néfastes de l'année égyptienne: traduction complète du Papyrus Sallier IV*. Paris: Maisonneuve.

Chalus, P. 1952 Foreword to Hubert 1952.

Chambers, E. K. 1903 *The Mediaeval Stage*, 2 vols. Oxford: Clarendon Press.

Cook, A. B. 1904 "The European Sky–God II." *Folk–lore* XV, 4: 369–426.

Czarnowski, S. 1919 *Le Culte des héros et ses conditions sociales. Saint Patrick, héros national de l'Irlande*. Paris: Alcan.

Drouin, H. 1929 "Henri Hubert." *Association de secours des anciens élèves de l'Ecole Normale Supérieure*: 45–51.

Duchesne, Abbé. 1898 *Premiers temps de l'Etat pontifical*. Paris: Fontemoing.

Duine, F. 1904 "Coutumes et superstitions de la Haute–Bretagne." *Revue des traditions populaires,* XIX: 112–14.

Durkheim, E. 1899 "De la Définition des phénomènes religieux." *L'Année sociologique,* II: 1–29.

Durkheim, E. and M. Mauss. 1903 "De quelques Formes primitives de classification, contribution à l'étude des représentations collectives." *L'Année sociologique,* V1: 1–72.

Durkheim, E. 1912 *Les Formes élémentaires de la vie religieuse.* Paris: Alcan.

Fowler, W. W. 1899 *The Roman Festivals of the Period of the Republic.* London: Macmillan.

Fraisse, P. 1957 *Psychologie du temps.* Paris: Presses Universitaires de France.

Frazer, J. G. 1900 *The Golden Bough,* 3 vols., 2nd ed. London: Macmillan.

Graf, J. H. *Über Zahlenaberglauben insbesondere die Zahl 13.* Bern: Wyss.

Grimm, J. L. K. 1875–8 *Deutsche Mythologie,* 3 vols., 4th ed. Berlin: Dümmler.

Grossin, W. 1974 *Les Temps de la vie quotidienne.* Paris: Mouton.

Gummere, F. B. 1901 *The Beginnings of Poetry.* New York: Macmillan.

Gunkel, J. F. H. 1903 *Zum religions-geschichtlichen Verständniß des neuen Testaments.* Göttingen: Vandenhoeck & Ruprecht.

Gurvitch, G. 1950 Foreword to Mauss 1950.

Gurvitch, G. 1961 *La Multiplicité des temps sociaux.* Paris: Cours Documentation Université (Sorbonne). And in Gurvitch 1963.

Gurvitch. G. 1963 *La Vocation actuelle de la sociologie,* 2 vols. Paris: Presses Universitaires de France.

Guyau, J-M. 1890 *La genèse de l'idée de temps.* Paris: Alcan.

Guyot, N. 1904 "Le Folk–lore de la Côte d'Or." *Revue des traditions populaires,* XIX: 217–20.

Halbwachs, M. 1925 *Les Cadres sociaux de la mémoire.* Paris: Alcan.

Halbwachs, M. 1950 *Mémoire et société.* Paris: Presses Universitaires de France.

Harou, A. 1904 "Notes sur les traditions et légendes de la province de Liège." *Revue des traditions populaires,* XIX: 296–303.

Hartland, E. S. 1894–6 *The Legend of Perseus: A Study of Tradition in Story, Custom and Belief,* 3 vols. London: Nutt.

Heuillard, C. 1904 "Traditions et superstitions de la Champagne." *Revue des traditions populaires,* XIX: 22

Hull, E. 1901 "Old Irish Tabus, or *Geasa.*" *Folk–lore* XII, 1: 41–66.

Isambert, F-A. 1976 "L'Elaboration de la notion de sacré dans l'école durkheimienne." *Archives de sciences sociales des religions,* 42: 35–56.

Isambert, F.-A. 1979 "Henri Hubert et la sociologie du temps." *Revue française de sociologie,* XX, 1: 183–204.

Jankélévitch, V. 1931 *Bergson.* Paris: Alcan.

Kellner, K. 1906 *Heortologie; oder Die geschichtliche Entwicklung des Kirchenjahres und der Heiligenfeste von den ältesten Zeiten bis zur Gegenwart,* 2nd ed. Freiburg im Breisgau: Herder.

Kewitsch, G. 1904 "Zweifel an der astronomischen und geometrischen Grundlage des 60–Systems." *Zeitschift für Assyriologie und vorderasiatische Archäologie,* XIX: 73–95.

Kluge, F. 1883 *Etymologisches Wörterbuch der deutschen Sprache*. Strassburg: Trübner.

Kluge, F. and F. Lutz 1898 *English Etymology: A Select Glossary*. Strassburg: Trübner.

Lagrange, M. J. 1905 *Etudes sur les religions sémitiques*, 2nd ed. Paris: Lecoffre.

Lantier, R. 1928 "Hommage à Henri Hubert et bibliographie d'Henri Hubert." *Revue archéologique*, XVII, 2: 289–307.

Lévy-Bruhl, L. 1938 *L'Expérience mystique et les symboles chez les primitifs*. Paris: Alcan.

Lévi-Strauss, C. 1950 "Introduction à l'œuvre de Marcel Mauss." In M. Mauss, *Sociologie et anthropologie*. Paris: Presses Universitaires de France.

McGee, W. J. 1900 "Primitive Numbers." *19th Annual Report of the Bureau of Ethnology* Part 2, [1897–8]: 821–51.

Mannhardt, J. W. E. 1858 *Germanische Mythen Forschungen*. Berlin: Schneider.

Mauss, M. 1903 Review of F. Gummere, *The Beginnings of Poetry. L'Année sociologique*, VI: 560–5.

Mauss, M. 1904 "L'Origine des pouvoirs magiques dans les sociétés australiennes." *Annuaire de l'Ecole Pratique des Hautes Etudes*, Section des Sciences religieuses: 1–55. Reprinted in Hubert and Mauss 1909a.

Mauss, M. 1907 Review of H. Hubert, "Etude sommaire de la représentation du temps dans la religion et la magie." *L'Année sociologique*, X: 302–304.

Mauss, M. 1930 "Les Civilisations. Eléments et formes." *Le mot et l'idée,* 1re Semaine internationale de synthèse, Paris: 99-100.

Mauss, M. 1932 Preface to Hubert 1932.

Mauss, M. 1950 *Sociologie et anthropologie*. Paris: Presses Universitaires de France.

Mauss, M. 1968 *Œuvres,* 3 vols., edited by V.Karady. Paris: Editions de Minuit.

Meyer, E. 1904–1907 *Ægyptische Chronologie.* Berlin: Verlag der Königl. Akademie der Wissenschaften.

Meyer, E. H. 1903 *Mythologie der Germanen gemeinfaßlich dargestellt.* Strassburg: Trübner.

Müller, K. O. 1824 *Die Dorier,* Breslau: Max.

Nore, A. de [= Adolphe de Chesnel]. 1846 *Coutumes, mythes et traditions des provinces de France.* Paris: Périsse.

Paul, H. 1896–7. "Mal." *Deutsches Wörterbuch.* Halle: Niemeyer.

Peal, S. E. 1899 "Ein Ausflug nach Banpara", *Zeitschrift für Ethnologie,* XXX: 281–371.

Pineau, L. 1904 "Le Folk-lore de la Touraine, VI." *Revue des traditions populaires,* XIX: 293–5.

Pinza, G. 1898 *La conservazione delle teste umane e le idee ed i costumi coi quali si connette.* Rome: Società geografica italiana.

Pitrè, G. 1900 *Feste patronali in Sicilia.* Torino and Palermo: Clausen.

Rawlinson, H. C. 1861–84 *The Cuneiform Inscriptions of Western Asia,* 5 vols., 2nd ed. London: British Museum.

Reinach, S. 1927 "Henri Hubert." *Revue archéologique,* XVII: 176–178.

Rhys, J. 1901 *Celtic Folklore: Welsh and Manx,* 2 vols. Oxford: Clarendon Press.

Roscher, W. H. 1903 *Die enneadischen und hebdo-madischen Fristen und Wochen der ältesten Griechen, ein Beitrag zur vergleichenden Chronologie und Zahlen mystik.* Leipzig: Teubner.

Saintyves, P. 1919 "Les notions de temps et d'éternité dans la magie et la religion." *Revue de l'histoire des religions,* 179: 75–104.

Sapper, K. 1904 "Religiöse Gebräuche der Kekchi–Indianer." *Archiv für Religionswissenschaft,* VII, 3–4: 453–70.

Schürer, E. 1890. *Geschichte des jüdischen Volkes im Zeitalter Jesu Christi,* 2nd ed. Leipzig: Hinrichs.

Sébillot, P. Y. 1904–7 *Le Folk-lore de France,* 4 vols. Paris: Guilmoto.

Strenski, I. 1987 "Henri Hubert, Racial Science and Political Myth." *Journal of the History of Behavorial Sciences,* 23: 353–367.

Strenski, I. 1991 "Hubert, Mauss and the Comparative Social History of Religions." In M. Despland, ed., *La Tradition française en sciences religieuses.*

Thompson, R. C. 1900 *The Reports of the Magicians and Astronomers of Nineveh and Babylon in the British Museum,* 2 vols. London: Luzac.

Tille, F. A. 1899 *Yule and Christmas: Their Place in the Germanic Year.* London: Nutt.

Varagnac, A. 1963 "Au musée des antiquités nationales, la rétrospective Broglie, Hubert et Mauss." *Antiquités nationales et internationales,* janv.–mars: 1–24.

Vendryès, J. 1927 "Henri Hubert." *Revue Celtique:* 500–502.

Weber, A. F. 1859 *Zwei vedische Texte über Omina und Portenta.* Berlin: Königl. Akademie der Wissenschaften.

Weber, A. F. (ed.). 1885 "Drittes Buch der Atharva–Samhita." *Indische Studien,* XVII, 2–3: 177–314.

Weber, A. F. 1898 "Vedische Beiträge." *Sitzungsberichte d. kgl. pr. Ak. d. Wiss. zu Berlin,* XXXVII: 558–81.

Winckler, H. 1904 "Die Weltanschauung des alten Orients." *Ex Oriente Lux,* I, 1: 1–50.

Wünsch, R. 1902 *Das Frühlingsfest der Insel Malta: ein Beitrag zur Geschichte der Antiken Religion.* Leipzig: Teubner.

Wuttke, K. F. A. 1869 *Der deutsche Volksaberglaube der Gegenwart,* 2nd ed. Berlin: Wiegand & Grieben.